CATHOLIC
FAITH *in* AMERICA

CHESTER GILLIS

J. GORDON MELTON, SERIES EDITOR

Facts On File, Inc.

CATHOLIC FAITH IN AMERICA
Faith in America

Facts On File, Inc.
132 West 31st Street
New York NY 10001

Library of Congress Cataloging-in-Publication Data

Gillis, Chester, 1951–
      Catholic faith in America / Chester Gillis.
        p.cm. — (Faith in America)
      Includes bibliographical references (p.) and index.
      ISBN 0-8160-4984-X
       1. Catholic Church—United States—History. 2. United States--Church history. I. Title. II. Series

      BX1406.3 .G55 2002
      282'.73—dc21   2002028590

Facts On File books are available at special discounts when purchased in bulk quantities for businesses, associations, institutions, or sales promotions. Please call our Special Sales Department in New York at (212) 967-8800 or (800) 322-8755.

You can find Facts On File on the World Wide Web at http://www.factsonfile.com

Produced by the Shoreline Publishing Group LLC
Editorial Director: James Buckley Jr.
Contributing Editor: Beth Adelman
Designed by Thomas Carling, Carling Design, Inc.
Index by Nanette Cardon, IRIS

Photo and art credits:
Cover: AP/Wide World (3); Photodisc (bottom center). AP/Wide World: 31, 33, 41, 45, 49, 73, 85, 87, 90, 98, 105, 106, 107, 109, 111, 113; Art Resource: 9, 18; Catholic News Service: 68, 76, 93; Courtesy Catholic Worker Los Angeles: 81; Courtesy Tom Carling: 55; Corbis: 26, 52, 116; Digital Stock: 6, 13, 16; Mike Eliason: 38; Courtesy EWTN: 63; Courtesy Marquette University: 94.

Dedication: For Alison, God's grace incarnate.

Printed in the United States of America

VB 10 9 8 7 6 5 4 3 2 1

This book is printed on acid-free paper.

CONTENTS

Foreword by J. Gordon Melton 4

INTRODUCTION Catholic Beliefs and Practices 7

CHAPTER 1 Catholic America: Then and Now 19

CHAPTER 2 Important American Catholic Events 39

CHAPTER 3 Catholic Impact on American Culture 53

CHAPTER 4 Catholic Impact on Social Issues 69

CHAPTER 5 Catholics and American Politics 85

CHAPTER 6 Important American Catholics 95

CHAPTER 7 Catholic America: What Is Next? 111

Glossary 120

Time Line 122

Resources 123

Index 124

FOREWORD

AMERICA BEGINS A NEW MILLENNIUM AS ONE OF THE MOST RELIGIOUSLY diverse nations of all time. Nowhere else in the world do so many people—offered a choice free from government influence—identify with such a wide range of religious and spiritual communities. Nowhere else has the human search for meaning been so varied. In America today, there are communities and centers for worship representing all of the world's religions.

The American landscape is dotted with churches, temples, synagogues, and mosques. Zen Buddhist zendos sit next to Pentecostal tabernacles. Hasidic Jews walk the streets with Hindu swamis. Most amazing of all, relatively little conflict has occurred among religions in America. This fact, combined with a high level of tolerance of one another's beliefs and practices, has let America produce people of goodwill ready to try to resolve any tensions that might emerge.

The Faith in America series celebrates America's diverse religious heritage. People of faith and ideals who longed for a better world have created a unique society where freedom of religious expression is a keynote of culture. The freedom that America offers to people of faith means that not only have ancient religions found a home here, but that newer forms of expressing spirituality have also taken root. From huge churches in large cities to small spiritual communities in towns and villages, faith in America has never been stronger. The paths that different religions have taken through American history is just one of the stories readers will find in this series.

Like anything people create, religion is far from perfect. However, its contribution to the culture and its ability to help people are impressive, and these accomplishments will be found in all the books in the series. Meanwhile, awareness and tolerance of the different paths our neighbors take to the spiritual life has become an increasingly important part of citizenship in America.

Today, more than ever, America as a whole puts its faith in freedom—the freedom to believe.

Catholic Faith in America

Although America is sometimes thought of as a Protestant nation, the single largest religious body in the country is the Roman Catholic Church. It remains a church led by bishops, archbishops, and the pope, but the Catholic Church has adapted to American life and the demands of a democratic society. The Church in America has prospered as one minority in a land where no single religious group is the majority.

The story of the Roman Catholic Church is most important for the 23 percent of the population raised as Catholics. But the way that the Church struggled to survive in the New World is interesting for all. How does an ancient organization and its people come to terms with a fast-moving culture in love with the discoveries of science? How does a group made of many different sorts of people reach consensus through the clash of opposing opinions? How does a group led from far-off Rome value the participation of the faithful in the running of its institutions?

Catholicism has been a big part of American public life. Catholics have held responsible positions in government at every level, including the highest office in the land. They have entertained us on stage and screen, pioneered social reform, and called the public to an ethical life. Catholics have championed efforts for world peace, and hundreds of thousands have served in the armed services. Some choose to spend their life serving the poor, the ill, and the outcast, while others manage large corporations. *Catholic Faith in America* explores these many facets of Catholic life. It opens a door into this faith's beliefs and practices, and its members' education and ethical development, while pointing the reader to the many places where Catholics contribute every day to the development of the American nation.

— *J. Gordon Melton, Series Editor*

INTRODUCTION

Catholic Beliefs and Practices

CATHOLICS IN AMERICA PARTICIPATE IN THE CHRISTIAN RELIGION that originated approximately 2,000 years ago and has the largest worldwide following of all religions. Catholic Christians, who number 1 billion worldwide, trace their roots directly to the earliest followers of Jesus Christ, after whom Christianity is named. Although some people mistakenly refer to Jesus as a Christian, he was a Jew who lived in Israel in the first century. Christians date their calendar from the time of his birth in Bethlehem, a calendar that has been adopted as a common measure of time across the globe.

Jesus was a teacher who attracted a number of followers during his 33-year lifetime. For most of his life, he remained a relatively unknown figure, but at about the age of 30, he began to preach publicly a message that the reign of God was at hand and that people should repent their sins and transform their lives in accordance with God's will.

At the time when Jesus preached, the Jews in Israel lived under the rule of the Roman Empire and had limited rights. During their long history in the region, the Jews developed an expectation that a Messiah (the word means "anointed one"; anointed means one chosen for a special purpose) would be sent by God to lead the Jewish people out of persecution and into freedom. Early followers of Jesus began to identify him as this Messiah.

Others thought he was just another wise teacher, or perhaps an earlier prophet such as Jeremiah, Isaiah, or Micah.

Jesus began his public ministry of teaching, preaching, and healing when he was baptized by John the Baptist, who had a group of followers before Jesus became a public figure. John recognized Jesus as greater than himself and yielded spiritual authority to him. Then Jesus began to gather followers around him, usually drawn from among the poor. Twelve of Jesus' followers became his closest disciples, and he called them to follow him regularly and faithfully. They became known as the Twelve Apostles. These were Jesus' most intimate followers, but a larger group called simply disciples began to follow him as well.

For about three years Jesus taught them, often by using stories called parables that always seemed to have a twist in them so that what the hearer of the story might expect did not happen. Many of these parables are well known in America, even to non-Christians.

For example, Jesus told a parable of the lost sheep, a story in which a shepherd left his entire flock alone in order to seek out and find one wandering sheep. Jesus used the parable to teach his followers that God would care in a special way for those who were spiritually lost. Also, he taught that every individual was important and worth saving in God's eyes.

Jesus' teachings attracted many followers, but also upset people. He often challenged those with religious or political power. Jewish teachers as well as Roman officials began to oppose him. Jesus empowered the poor, performed miraculous acts, and even forgave sinners, a privilege the Jews believed was reserved only for God. Many began to question by whose authority he could do these things. Jesus said his authority came from God, but many did not believe him and they either thought he was a foolish pretender whom they could ignore or that he was dangerous.

Eventually, the Roman authorities decided to put a stop to his teaching. After one of his own apostles, Judas, betrayed Jesus, the Romans arrested Jesus, tried him, and put him to death by hanging him on a cross outside the ancient city of Jerusalem. His followers, then and now, believe that God raised Jesus from the dead. Christians today celebrate this event each spring as Easter. Followers also believe that he taught for another 40 days after coming back, before returning for good to God in heaven.

A dramatic calling
The man who would become one of Jesus' most important early followers was "converted" to belief in Christ rather suddenly. As this painting depicts, Paul was struck down from his horse by a bolt of lightning as he traveled, according to the story, "on the road to Damascus [Syria.]"

The Early Church

Soon after the death and resurrection of Jesus, various communities of followers began to meet together to pray and to follow his example. Some of these were Jews and some were Gentiles (non-Jews). In the decades immediately following Jesus' death, resurrection, and ascension into heaven, a Jew named Saul, a member of a Jewish religious group called Pharisees, was dramatically converted to Christianity. Renamed Paul, he began to organize various communities into churches. Paul visited communities in the Middle East, from Greece to Israel. He also wrote letters to them to encourage their commitment to Jesus' teachings and to help them resolve disputes. Approximately 40 years after Jesus' death, an early Christian named Mark wrote the first gospel about Jesus' life and what that life meant to those who follow Jesus. The word gospel means "good news," and Mark, who is known as an evangelist because he wrote a gospel, was telling the good news about Jesus Christ as God and savior. His gospel is not a biography since it begins with Jesus being baptized by John in the Jordan River when Jesus was about 30 years old. Mark did not intend to write a biography, but a reflection in faith on who Jesus was and what he did. His gospel was followed by other

The Creed

Basic Catholic beliefs are expressed in the Nicene Creed. This statement of beliefs dates back to a major Church gathering called the Council of Nicea in 325. The Creed was changed slightly by the Council of Constantinople in 381. Catholics continue to recite this creed today in the liturgy, or mass, as the church has done since the 11th century.

We believe in one God,
the Father, the Almighty.
maker of heaven and earth,
of all that is seen and unseen.
We believe in one Lord, Jesus Christ, the only Son of God,
eternally begotten of the Father,
God from God, Light from Light,
true God from true God,
begotten, not made, one in Being with the Father,
Through him all things were made,
For us men and for our salvation
he came down from heaven:
by the power of the Holy Spirit
he was born of the Virgin Mary, and became man.
For our sake he was crucified under Pontius Pilate,
he suffered, died, and was buried.
On the third day he rose again
in fulfillment of the Scriptures;
he ascended into heaven
and is seated at the right hand of the Father.
He will come again in glory to judge the living and the dead,
and his kingdom will have no end.
We believe in the Holy Spirit, the Lord, the giver of life,
who proceeds from the Father and the Son.
With the Father and the Son he is worshiped and glorified.
He has spoken through the prophets.
We believe in one, holy, catholic, and apostolic Church.
We acknowledge one baptism for the forgiveness of sins.
We look for the resurrection of the dead,
and the life of the world to come. Amen.

gospels written by Matthew, Luke, and John. The evangelists received their information about Jesus from some of the eyewitnesses to Jesus' ministry. Although the gospels have many similarities, they nevertheless are marked by differences, showing that each evangelist was writing for a different audience and wanted to stress different aspects of Jesus' life and ministry. For example, only Matthew and Luke's gospels describe Jesus' birth (on the holiday now called Christmas) with details that link Jesus to the fulfillment of the Jewish expectations for the Messiah. However, all of the gospels are intended to both witness to the faith in Jesus that his followers had and to invite others into that faith. Paul's letters, sometimes called epistles, and the four Gospels eventually were collected along with other significant texts, and became the New Testament. Christians refer to the 27 books of the New Testament of the Bible as "the word of God." They also consider the Old Testament to be sacred books that, although written by humans, are inspired by God.

From these early beginnings, the church developed into a complex organization. As the number of Christians grew, the need for organization also grew. By the second century, leaders of the church emerged. They led Christians in prayer, organized the various communities that were emerging, and made rules about the beliefs and practices of Christians. Certain persons were designated to perform these functions, and the priesthood emerged. Then some, known as bishops, were given special responsibilities to oversee the priests and the churches as spiritual leaders and administrators. All of this occurred in the first three centuries of the church's existence.

Among the twelve Apostles, Peter performed a special role as a leader since Jesus said to him: "You are Peter [a name that means "rock"] and upon this rock I will build my church." Catholics trace the leadership of their church all the way back to Saint Peter, so that the pope, who is the successor to Peter as the bishop of Rome, is considered the head of the church. The church developed a strong structure of central authority, making it what is known as a hierarchical church (meaning it has a chain of command with the pope at the top).

In the year 314, the Roman emperor, Constantine, decided to unify his kingdom under the banner of one religion, Christianity. Under Constantine's leadership most of the empire converted to Christianity. In the year 325, the church leaders held an meeting called the Council of Nicea (after the place where it was held in what is today Turkey) in which

HONORING MARY
The U.S. Postal Service issues a stamp every Christmas usually with an image of Mary and Jesus (known as "the Madonna and child") taken from a famous painting.

Seven Sacraments

Baptism: When a person is initiated into the Church. Water is poured on them in some way. The phrase "In the name of the Father, Son, and Holy Spirit" is used. This is usually performed on infants, but adults can be baptized, too.

Reconciliation: Also know as Penance or Confession. Believers meet with a priest and describe sins they are sorry they committed. The priest, speaking for God, forgives those sins and advises how to avoid them in the future.

Eucharist: The eating of bread and drinking of wine that Catholics believe has become the body and blood of Christ (see page 16).

Confirmation: An additional ritual of initiation, usually taken as a teenager.

Marriage: The joining of a man and woman as husband and wife.

Holy Orders: When a man becomes a priest, deacon, or bishop.

Anointing of the Sick: Special prayers for very sick people; formerly only performed on dying people.

they proclaimed certain beliefs of the church as necessary for Christians to hold. Specifically, they made clear that the church believed that Jesus was both God and man in one person. Before this council, different groups in the church disputed exactly what they believed about Jesus Christ. From then on, those who did not believe that he was God and human were considered heretics (wrong in their belief). In 425, the church held another meeting, called the Council of Chalcedon, that further defined the beliefs of the church and that Christians were required to believe to remain in good standing with the church.

The Church's Influence Grows

As the church developed and refined its beliefs and practices internally, it also spread across many lands and began to influence all of Western culture. The Catholic Church, with its strong organization and well-defined beliefs, attracted many converts and influenced various dimensions of social and cultural life such as art, music, architecture, government, and law. To confirm this, all one has to do is stroll through any museum in Europe and look at what most of the great art depicts: paintings of events in Jesus' life such as his birth or his death on the cross, sculptures of Mary and Jesus, frescoes depicting angels and heavenly scenes, as well as elaborate cathedrals filled with priceless Christian art.

The Catholic Church wielded enormous influence on society,

with medieval kings and queens often being crowned by cardinals (a group of the pope's special advisors who are above bishops) or the pope himself. Although Americans can hardly imagine our president taking an oath of loyalty to the pope or being installed by the local bishop, presidents still place their hand on the Bible when they take their oath of office and the ceremony includes a prayer.

Catholic Beliefs and Practices

Christians believe that Jesus was both God and human at the same time. This belief, among others, distinguishes Christianity from other world religions (for example, Judaism and Islam) that do not claim that God became human in a single, unique person. Further, Christians believe that Jesus' death on the cross was an act that saved humanity from the consequences of its sins. Jesus is the way to God, they believe.

Over many centuries of its existence the church clarified its be-

Mary, mother of God
More than most Christian faiths, Catholics hold Mary, the mother of Jesus, in a place of special regard. They believe that she gave birth to Jesus and yet remained a virgin, a miracle Christians believe sets her apart from other women. Special prayers are said to Mary, who is also the patroness, or special protector, of America.

liefs, formalized its rituals, and specified practices for its members to follow. Thus, by about the year 1200 the church settled on seven sacraments as central to Catholic spiritual life (see box on page 12). Sacraments are rituals that Catholics participate in which are intended to bring them closer to God. They believe that sacraments bring them God's grace (a share in God's life), so they represent a very important dimension of Catholic spiritual life and Catholics consider them sacred events that help them to be holy.

Most Catholics are baptized as infants, although one can receive this sacrament, which is only conferred once in an individual's lifetime, as an adult. This sacrament initiates Catholics into the Christian life, but it is the Eucharist (pronounced "*YOUK-uh-rist*," the word means "thanksgiving"), the sacrament of the body and blood of Christ, that sustains Catholics in their spiritual life. The Catholic Church teaches that the bread and wine that Catholics receive in Communion (another term for Eucharist) has been transformed within the ritual of the Mass presided over by a priest into the actual body and blood of Jesus Christ. The bread and wine do not change in appearance, but in

The Protestant Reformation

In the 16th century a movement occurred that resulted in the creation of Protestant Christianity. Led initially by Martin Luther in 1517, a German priest within the Catholic Church who objected publicly to what he considered dubious church practices, the Protestant movement developed from its beginnings in Germany into several different expressions of Christianity. Shortly after Luther, John Calvin led a group of protesters in Geneva, who developed their own form of Protestantism. Today, a variety of Protestant churches count millions of Americans among their number. These include Lutherans, Methodists, and Presbyterians, among others.

Protestant Christianity differs from Catholic Christianity in practices and beliefs. They do not acknowledge the pope as their head; they generally have fewer sacraments (most only baptism and Eucharist); clergy are permitted to marry and women may be ordained; they emphasize the Bible and preaching; their churches are less hierarchical; and Mary and the saints are not revered in the same way that they are in Catholicism.

These are among the differences that separate them from Catholics, but there are also theological and practical differences that distinguish them from each other. Some have a formal worship style and others less formal, some have bishops while others do not, and some have uniform rules and beliefs while others allow individuals or congregations to be independent.

substance they are no longer merely bread and wine but the body and blood of the savior. The technical term for this is "transubstantiation."

Disputes over this and other teachings, as well as over issues of how the church should be run, led Protestants to break away from the Roman Catholic Church in the 16th century in a movement called the Reformation (see the box on page 14). Since that time there are different denominations, or versions, of Christianity in the West (for example, Lutheran, Methodist, Presbyterian, and Baptist). Much earlier (in the year 1046) the Catholic Church split into Eastern and Western divisions. Orthodox Catholics with Eastern roots (Greek and Russian, for example) are found in the United States, as well as Roman Catholics (see the box on page 25).

One of the sacraments that Catholics celebrate about which non-Catholics sometimes know very little, or which they find mysterious, is the sacrament of Reconciliation, commonly called Confession. Everyone needs forgiveness at different times in their lives, such as when one has offended a parent, a spouse, a friend, or sometimes even a stranger. This sacrament encourages Catholics to ask forgiveness of God and of their neighbors. The priest acts as an intermediary, reconciling sinners to God. In the name of the Church and in God's name the priest offers absolution (forgiveness) to sinners who are sorry for their sins and who ask to be forgiven. God's forgiveness is without end, so no sin is too terrible to be forgiven, and one can receive this sacrament an unlimited number of times in one's life.

Sacraments and the Mass

The Eucharist is usually received during the liturgy (the Church's official worship) of the Eucharist, or Mass. Mass is celebrated daily in most Catholic churches in America and around the world. Catholics are required by church law to participate at Mass on Sundays, a special day of prayer. Not all Catholics go to church every Sunday, but many do. Sundays are bustling with activity as Catholic churches provide a schedule of Masses that begins on Saturday night (anticipating, and thus counting as, Sunday worship) and moves throughout the day on Sunday.

Catholics worship at and belong to parishes, which are individual churches that serve a specific group of Catholics, usually determined by the neighborhoods where they live. Parishes constitute smaller

CONFESSION AND U.S. LAW

Catholics have the choice of confessing their sins to the priest face to face or in the secrecy of the confessional booth from behind a screen that masks their identity. Priests are bound by a sacred oath not to disclose anything that is revealed to them in this sacrament. American courts have respected this "seal of confession" by not forcing priests to disclose what they have heard in confession, even if that might be evidence of a crime. The seal of confession is similar to the bond between a doctor and patient or a lawyer and client.

Do this in memory of me
The Eucharist at Catholic Mass recalls the Last Supper, when Jesus ate with his disciples for the final time before his death. In this ritual, Catholics believe that the bread or wafer is changed into the body of Christ. By consuming it, Catholics take part in his life.

Catholic communities where people can form bonds, serve the needs of their membership, and reach out to the larger community. Catholics who are active in their faith center their religious life within the parish. Parishes are headed by a priest who is the pastor. He may be assisted by another priest, a nun, a deacon (an ordained layman one step below the priesthood), and laity. In recent years the church has suffered a shortage of priests, so nuns administer some parishes. A collection of parishes in a geographical area makes up a diocese over which a bishop or archbishop presides.

Prayers, Saints, and Mary

Rituals play an important role in the spiritual lives of Catholics, but they are not the exclusive form of prayer. Catholics also recite well-known prayers like the Our Father and Hail Mary. These are are also part of the rosary, a prayer cycle aided by a string of 59 beads on which one counts the prayers. The string is often connected to a small crucifix, or cross with the body of Jesus on it. They read the Bible, pray in small groups, go on spiritual retreats, and offer blessings before meals.

One figure whom Catholics revere is Mary, the mother of Jesus.

She holds a special place in the hearts of many Catholics and the church honors her with more titles than Jesus. Catholics pray for her help in connecting with her Son and with God. She represents both humility and strength. Her humility is shown when she willingly and gracefully accepts God's will for her. Her strength is revealed as the mother of a son who she gives to be crucified. American Catholics honor her as the Patroness of America and celebrate her feast on December 8 each year.

Saints also abound in the Catholic tradition. The church singles out these noble figures for their heroic example as model followers of Christ. Over the centuries the church has sanctified many people with this honor, among them a handful of Americans. Some of their stories are told in chapter 6.

A Universal Church

American Catholics identify with a universal church, headquartered in Rome under the direction of the pope. This gives them a common identity with Catholics worldwide. Although authors and television news commonly use the phrase "the American Catholic Church," they actually are referring to "the Roman Catholic Church in America" because American Catholics are tied to authorities in Rome, in particular the pope.

Many non-Catholics seem to be puzzled by this relationship that all Catholics have with the pope. The pope, as the successor to Saint Peter, exercises a special responsibility for the universal church. In this role he enjoys worldwide recognition as the best-known religious leader. He also exerts his influence over Catholics everywhere, including American Catholics. He appoints bishops and cardinals, issues laws and regulations, sets ethical standards, and speaks out on issues that affect Catholics and populations at large. Since the Vatican, the pope's headquarters in Rome, is a state, the pope maintains diplomatic relations with most world leaders and often speaks forcefully for justice in parts of the world where people are oppressed.

While all American Catholics are under the direction of the Vatican in Rome, nevertheless, Roman Catholics in America enjoy a unique history and an identity that distinguishes them from other Catholics in the world, as we will see in the next chapter.

CATHOLIC CHURCH TITLES

MALE

Pope: Leader of all Catholics worldwide

Cardinal: High official, often in charge of a major diocese (Note: Only those with the rank of Cardinal, and who are less than 80 years old, can vote to elect a new pope.)

Archbishop: A senior bishop

Bishop: The man in charge of a diocese

Monsignor: An honorary title for a senior priest

Priest: A man ordained with the powers of a priest; called "Father"

Monk: A type of priest who lives in a monastery, or special place of faith and work

Deacon: A person ordained for special duties and powers in the church

FEMALE

Mother Superior: A senior nun in charge of a group of nuns

Nun: A woman professed to a life in the church; often called "Sister"

Catholic America: Then and Now

CATHOLICS LIVED IN AMERICA FOR CENTURIES BEFORE THE colonial period. Priests from religious orders (special communities dedicated to particular works) established Catholic communities in the 16th and 17th centuries. These priests, who were mostly Spanish Jesuits and Franciscans, converted numerous people in the regions that would later be known as Florida, Texas, New Mexico, Arizona, Louisiana, and California, giving Catholicism deep roots in America. These early Catholic missionary priests established the famous Spanish missions in California (see page 39). The Church established a diocese in the U.S. territory of Puerto Rico in 1511, the oldest diocese in U.S. territory. Spanish colonies also were set up in southern Florida for a short time and Catholic priests established places of worship there.

In Canada and parts of what is now the northern midwest of America, French missionary priests did the same thing, living among and working with various Native American tribes in an effort to turn them into Catholic Christians. Two French Jesuits became saints and martyrs (people killed because of their beliefs) when their efforts to convert Huron and Mohawk tribes were met with resistance and the missionaries were killed.

As European colonists, primarily from Great Britain, began to come across the Atlantic in the early 1600s, Protestants comprised the most influential religious group. They came to New England from Great Britain to establish colonies that eventually became the first states. Many of these early settlers left Britain, which had a state religion that favored certain Christians over others, because they wanted greater religious freedom. Ironically, the colonists also favored certain religious groups and even established their own state religions. For one thing, since Puritans wanted to cleanse Christianity from its ties to the pope, Catholics were unwelcome in most of the early colonies.

Orthodox Christianity arrived about this time, too. Priests and monks from the Russian Orthodox Church traveled for 293 days from St. Petersburg, Russia, to Kodiak, Alaska. They arrived on September 24 ,1794, and founded the Russian Orthodox Church in America.

A Home in Maryland

During the early colonial period, Maryland was the one place where Catholics found acceptance. On March 5, 1634, a group of them arrived in Maryland aboard the *Ark* and the *Dove*, the ships that transported them from England. They established Saint Mary's City, the first capital of Maryland and a safe haven for Catholics. Among the Catholic settlers in Maryland, some distinguished noblemen, in particular the Calvert family, aided significantly in establishing Catholicism in this colony. They also brought slaves with them, many of whom were Catholic as well. Other colonies that allowed their communities to practice their own religions were Rhode Island and Pennsylvania. Roger Williams, a Baptist, founded Rhode Island, and William Penn, a Quaker, created Pennsylvania.

Maryland Catholics endured many hardships while trying to practice their faith. At the beginning of the 18th century Catholics accounted for only about 10 percent of the population in Maryland. The Jesuits priests were few in number, enjoyed few privileges from the state, and generally lived and worked on plantations. Some moved from town to town preaching and bringing the sacraments to Catholics dispersed throughout the region. Nuns from a variety of religious orders based in Europe also ministered among these pioneer Catholics. The state left them alone if they kept their activities private and did not aggressively recruit converts.

In 1789 John Carroll became the first bishop of an American diocese, in Baltimore. In the same year he founded Georgetown

PRECEDING PAGE
America's first bishop
The first major leader of the Catholic Church in America was Bishop John Carroll (1735–1815). Born in Maryland and educated in Europe, Carroll helped found several important Catholic institutions and helped get the church established in the new United States.

University, a Jesuit institution and the oldest Catholic university in America. Carroll came from a prominent family that included his brother, Daniel, who was involved with the Continental Congress and who was one of two Catholics to sign the U.S. Constitution. Their cousin, Charles, enjoyed the distinction of being the only Catholic to sign the Declaration of Independence. Bishop Carroll was elected by the priests and approved by the Vatican. Today, bishops are not elected but are appointed directly by the Vatican.

Numbers Increase

From these humble beginnings the number of Catholics in America began to grow, and yet Catholics were still discriminated against by the powerful Protestant majority. By the time of Bishop Carroll's death in 1815, the Catholic Church was firmly grounded in America. The church's growth involved struggle, however.

In addition to encountering religious prejudice, the vast majority of Catholics came from among the lower class, which meant that they had neither economic might nor political influence. However, their numbers increased as immigrants from Europe poured into the United States beginning in the 18th century, led by the Irish, who fled the potato famine that starved Ireland. Irish Catholics became the dominant force within the Catholic Church in America, populating the pews and the seminaries (schools to train priests).

Irish Immigrants

Irish Catholics comprise one of the largest segments of the American Church. Ireland is a heavily Catholic country that is thriving today as a member of the European Union. But from 1846 to 1850 the Irish suffered one of the worst famines in European history. Irish farmers depended almost exclusively on their potato crop for survival. In 1846 the potatoes became diseased with a blight that virtually wiped out the entire crop. The blight lasted for five years, and hunger wiped out entire villages. Most Irish farmers did not own their own land and usually used their harvest to pay their debts to the British Protestant landowners. The potato harvest both fed them and supported their livelihood, so when the crops failed they were desperate. Tens of thousands of Irish peasants died. In total, the famine claimed the lives of almost 1 million Irish citizens.

CATHOLICS AND SLAVERY
Ironically, like others at the time, the Jesuits, other religious orders, and some bishops owned slaves. In 1839, the Vatican objected to this practice and the Church abandoned the custom of holding slaves. Nevertheless, many Catholics clung to racist views. Religious orders such as the Josephite Fathers and Brothers and nuns of the Community of the Holy Family were established in the 1870s to minister within the African-American Catholic communities in cities such as New Orleans and Baltimore.

Having lost their crops, and thus their ability to pay their debts, the farmers were kicked out by landlords. Hundreds of thousands of Irish peasants then crowded the cities looking for work. All that was available to them were workhouses as overrun with disease and misery as the farms they had left. Some, who thought themselves fortunate, had landlords pay their passage to another country. The crowded ships they boarded were barely seaworthy and came to be known as "coffin ships" on which many passengers died. Those who survived the journey arrived in their new country emaciated, weak, and penniless.

America proved to be a key destination for these ragged immigrants. Irish-Americans became a notable presence within the United States, and they were virtually all Catholic. This influx of Irish-Catholic immigrants into America shifted the balance. From 1850 on, Irish Catholics comprised the largest group among American Catholics.

After their life-threatening experience in Ireland, these Irish immigrants no longer wished to be farmers, so they took jobs as laborers in factories. As builders and longshoremen, police officers and fire fighters, eventually they helped form unions to represent workers. Politically they aligned themselves with the Democratic Party. They became a formidable force in local politics in many cities. They also tended to discriminate against those lower on the social scale. Thus, they treated blacks poorly and when other immigrant groups arrived after them, such as the Italians, they looked down on them as inferior.

Besides local politics, the one place that the Irish dominated was in the Catholic parishes. They had a language advantage over many other immigrants because they spoke English (although with an Irish accent). They established large parishes with schools, social halls, and cemeteries. The "Irish" parish was *the* parish in many cities and neighborhoods. They also brought clergy from Ireland with them who began to fill the ranks of the American priesthood. Over time they imported more clergy, since Ireland had plenty of priests and seminarians and many were willing to begin a new life in America. Eventually, the Church elevated many of these to the rank of bishop and the Irish tightened their grip on power within the church. They faced a strong backlash within the larger American culture that resented Irish Catholics with a particular dislike. Non-Catholic Americans feared that Irish-Americans harbored a greater loyalty to the pope than to their new homeland.

Immigrants All

By 1850 Catholicism comprised the largest single denomination (branch of Christianity) in the United States, with 1.5 million people. Even today, it is the largest, with more than 65 million people calling themselves Catholic. In the early days, however, their numbers did not translate into power or influence. The larger culture proved to be anti-Catholic, barring Catholics from professions, discriminating against them in housing and education, and making them an underclass.

Catholics were an immigrant community whose numbers and diversity swelled in the 19th century with the arrival of German, Polish, Italian, and other refugee Catholic groups from Europe, as well as French Canadians. Together, they developed a rich and complex Catholic subculture with institutions and opportunities that mirrored the larger culture.

The many languages they spoke and the different cultures they brought with them from their countries of origin distinguished these immigrant Catholic communities from each other. The Catholic Church here began to take on an American flavor that represented remarkable diversity but also some similarities. Many of the immigrant communities brought priests with them to America, so they operated here the way they had back home. Bishops established what were known as "national" parishes, meaning that they served particular nationalities. There were Polish parishes, Italian parishes, French parishes, and so forth, each using the language and customs of their native countries. In some areas these national parishes were located only a few blocks from each other in city neighborhoods. They provided services in the immigrants' native languages and helped them form a community in which they could be understood and welcomed.

This 19th-century pattern is being repeated in many urban and suburban areas today that are home to more recent immigrants from Spanish speaking countries, Asia, and Africa. In the Los Angeles Archdiocese today, Sunday Mass is celebrated in dozens of different languages. In addition, Orthodox churches include many immigrants from Eastern Europe and Russia among their congregations.

Not all immigrants spoke a foreign tongue, however. Irish Catholic immigrants were the largest and most influential group that settled in America. Since they spoke English, they adjusted to American society fairly quickly. The Irish immigrant community produced an extraordinary number of vocations to (or, decisions to join) the clergy. Many priests from Ireland also decided to come to America to work in a church that was considered missionary territory by the Vatican. While the national parishes were designed for non-English-speaking immigrants, Irish clergy staffed the territorial parishes, meaning the ordinary ones that served neighborhoods. Revered by their parishioners, they exercised a powerful influence in the American church. As a result, the vast majority of bishops came from the ranks of priests of Irish descent. To this day, most bishops are Irish-Americans.

Discrimination Against Catholics

Catholics did not have an easy time in America in the 19th and early 20th centuries. They generally held low paying jobs, had little political influence, and found themselves excluded from important social institutions and higher education. A political group known as the Know-Nothings formed in the South before the Civil War. They opposed the church and tormented Catholics. In the Midwest, an organization called the American Protective Association discriminated against Catholics. While best known for its racism against African-Americans, the Ku Klux Klan also targeted Catholics with its unique brand of hate. In early 20th-century Boston, Irish Catholics looking for work encountered signs in shop windows that read "No Irish Need Apply." It proved to be so common that the abbreviation NINA often replaced the full expression and everyone knew what it meant.

Protestants, called nativists because they first settled most of the colonies, dominated all of the important dimensions of society. Thus, America's finest universities, including Ivy League institutions such as Harvard and Yale, did not permit Catholics to enroll. They were barred from joining country clubs, living in certain neighborhoods, and holding significant positions in business, government, or industry. They were outsiders in their own adopted land. Although Congress appointed a priest as its chaplain in 1832, symbolizing Catholics' visibility within the society, it was not until 1998 that Congress again chose a Catholic to lead its prayers.

Since they were outsiders, Catholics built a subculture, a structure that could serve their needs. This subculture paralleled the larger culture and gave them a unique identity. This Catholic subculture reached its height in the 1950s, when Catholics participated in a host of organizations that afforded them professional and personal relationships with other Catholics.

Social organizations complemented these professional societies with the establishment of men's organizations such as the Knights of Columbus (founded in 1882) and women's organizations such as the National Council of Catholic Women (1920). Young people joined the Catholic Youth Organization (1930) because they were excluded from joining the YWCA or YMCA. To fulfill their spiritual needs, Catholics formed the Holy Name Society (1882) and the Rosary and Altar Society (1896). In other words, since they were largely excluded from organi-

Orthodox Christianity in America

During the late 19th century, Orthodox Christians arrived in America in significant numbers from Southern, Central and Eastern Europe, and the Balkans, from countries including Russia, Albania, Bulgaria, Belarus, Estonia, Georgia, Romania, Serbia, and Ukraine. They also came from Syria, Armenia, Lebanon, Egypt, and especially from Greece. (Estimates suggest that 600,000 Greeks arrived in the United States between 1890 and 1920.)

This has resulted in a variety of Orthodox Churches such as the Serbian Orthodox, the Russian Orthodox, and the Greek Orthodox. Many of their practices differ from Roman Catholics. These Christians follow a different rite, have their own hierarchy, use the language of their native countries in liturgy, admit both celibate and married men to priesthood, do not permit marriage between religions, and maintain strong family ties within the religion. Some of the churches follow the direction of the leadership in their home countries and others have established churches in America. Some are tied to Rome and the pope, and others do not recognize the authority of the pope but have their own leaders called patriarchs. Their church buildings have distinctive architecture, ornate paintings, and decorations.

In the aftermath of the collapse of Communism in Central and Eastern Europe, the resulting dislocation meant that some refugees found their way to the United States and others were aided financially by Orthodox Churches in America. In some of the post-communist societies, the Orthodox Church was both the most significant religious body as well as the largest non-governmental institution. An inter-Orthodox humanitarian organization was established with its headquarters in Maryland and field offices in Moscow, Tbilisi, and Belgrade. The organization worked with the World Council of Churches, the National Council of Churches of Christ in the U.S.A., and humanitarian agencies to address the needs of the post-Soviet Union states.

In 1994 the Orthodox community marked the 200th anniversary of the Orthodox faith in North America. There are about 6 million Orthodox Christians in America today.

THE AMERICAN RIVER GANGES.

THE PRIESTS AND THE CHILDREN.—[SEE PAGE 915.]

Fear of Catholics

Cartoonist Thomas Nast changed mitres, *the hats worn by bishops, into crocodile heads to show the fear that some Americans had of Catholics taking over schools and government. This is an example of the anti-Catholic feelings of the late 19th century.*

zations dominated by Protestants, Catholics created a separate culture in which they could participate.

This history of prejudice stretched into the 20th century. In 1949, Paul Blanchard wrote in his book *American Freedom and Catholic Power*:

> Unfortunately the Catholic people of the United States are not citizens but subjects in their own religious commonwealth. The [nonreligious] as well as the religious policies of their Church are made in Rome by an organization that is alien in spirit and control. ... They are compelled by the very nature of their Church's structure to accept nonreligious as well as religious policies that have been imposed upon them from abroad.

Things have changed since then. While many Catholic organizations still exist in some form, Catholics no longer need to join them because they are no longer excluded from organizations in America. The religious discrimination has all but disappeared. Because of this welcoming atmosphere in the wider community, quite a few of these Catholic organizations have disappeared and many of those that continue are smaller today.

Though little anti-Catholic prejudice exists today, the prejudice Catholics encountered both marginalized and inspired them. It helped them to form a more or less cohesive social unit, gave them a particular identity, and encouraged them to form organizations designed to serve their needs.

Misunderstood by Rome

Catholics not only struggled to be accepted and understood by Americans, they also had conflicts with the Vatican, which misunderstood them and wanted to exercise control over them. In the late 19th century, Pope Leo XIII worried that American Catholics and their bishops were forging a path independent from Rome. The pope was accustomed to the church enjoying certain privileges from European governments. The American system of government differed considerably from those found in Europe. Unlike in Europe, the church and state were independent of one another. The founders of America consciously sought to separate the two so that no one religion would be the state religion. The United States Constitution guaranteed freedom of religion.

However, the pope wanted the church in America to enjoy special privileges such as government financial support. He wrote in an 1895 Encyclical (special papal letter): "[The U.S. Church] would bring forth more abundant fruits if, in addition to liberty, she enjoyed the favor of the laws and the patronage of the public authority." However, from the beginning America was intended to be religiously diverse, with people free to choose their religion or not to profess any religion. This arrangement, known as a secular state, does not prevent anyone from practicing his or her religion. On the other hand, it does not make one faith the preferred religion of the country. Many of the original colonists fled England because the state endorsed one religion (Anglicanism) and discriminated against other Christian denominations and other religions. At all costs, they wanted to avoid this in their new land. As it turned out they did not fully avoid it as some of the original 13 American colonies endorsed one denomination at the expense of others.

Unsatisfied with the American response to his 1895 letter, Pope Leo XIII wrote another in 1899 to the American Catholic Church. In it he warned the American Catholics not to create a church independent of Rome. This strongly worded letter put an end to any notions among Catholics in America that they would be "American Catholics" and not "Roman Catholics in America." The American bishops took their orders from Rome and kept the church loyal to the pope. Leo XIII's successor, Pope Pius X, further strengthened papal authority when he warned the church not to adopt the ways of the modern world.

The leaders of the American church heeded Rome's warnings and led the Church in a direction that the Vatican wanted. Catholics were happy to "pay, pray, and obey," as the saying went. The American Catholic Church followed the rules and regulations set up by Rome and enforced by the American bishops. Americans Catholics were faithful and obedient and the church continued to flourish.

Hispanic Immigrants

Immigration continued to have a big impact on Catholics in America throughout the 1900s. For instance, Latino and Latina Catholics form a very important group within the Catholic Church in America today. The Hispanic population makes up about one quarter of the American church and the number grows each year. Since 1960, Hispanics have accounted for 71 percent of Catholic growth in the U.S. In Chicago more than 50 percent of the immigrant population comes from Latin America. Others have their roots in Cuba or in the U.S. commonwealth of Puerto Rico. Each represents a distinctive culture. The vast majority of the American Hispanic community is Catholic, although in recent years some have joined Protestant and Evangelical churches.

Many churches offer Mass in Spanish to accommodate this growing population. But more than language distinguishes them. In some dioceses where they constitute a large part of the church, such as some locations in California, all priests learn Spanish in order to minister more effectively to the community. Their attachment to holy artifacts like rosary beads, statues, candles, and saints' images gives them a special identity among American Catholics. The music for their liturgies is lively and the Masses are often crowded.

The American bishops began a Committee for the Spanish Speaking in 1944 under the inaugural direction of Archbishop Robert E. Lucey of San Antonio, Texas. Many in the Hispanic community there were poor, disorganized, and subject to mistreatment and discrimination in the United States. In response to the problems faced by this migrant community, the bishops planned to build parish centers. There they hoped to educate them and encourage them to be Catholics and become priests and nuns. They also wanted to provide better health care and develop leaders. The bishops approved regional centers reporting to San Antonio. Nevertheless, it was difficult for mostly English-speaking priests to reach the migrant worker population.

The Protestants were making the effort to do so, however. Baptist preachers organized a "Cotton Patch Crusade" with ministers accompanying migrant workers in the fields of West Texas. To counteract their efforts, Lucey sent maps of the locations of migrant workers to priests and other missionaries "so that spiritual services may be given to them and they may be kept from Protestant proselytizers [people who try to convince others to convert to a faith]." He also began programs to teach seminarians to speak Spanish and brought to America some Mexican priests to help this growing and underserved population. He brought priests and lay workers from the Southwest together with their counterparts from the North to discuss their common problems in ministering to migrant workers. Archbishop Lucey convinced the U.S. Labor Department to contact growers' associations and individual farmers to let the priests provide religious services for the workers. This action led to a national bishops' committee for migrant workers.

In their efforts to maintain the loyalty of migrant workers the Bishops' Committee for the Spanish Speaking prepared a kit to be distributed to the workers that included a picture of Our Lady of Guadalupe for the front door of migrants' quarters, carrying the inscription (in Spanish): "This is a Catholic home and Protestant propaganda [materials favorable to a cause] will not be admitted." Obviously the church knew that Catholics were converting to Protestant denominations in significant numbers. The Protestants, while perhaps not passing out kits, were rewarding the most promising with scholarships, with a view toward training them to be ministers among their own people or in other Latin American countries in the future.

The bishops recognized as early as the 1950s that the clergy could not minister adequately to this burgeoning population. Recruiting dedicated Catholics to this work that had "no particular glamour" was an uphill battle. In addition to guarding their continued loyalty to Catholicism, the church attempted to bring economic justice to the migrant workers, often going up against the powerful growers who exploited them as cheap labor, and sometimes defying the government.

A committee of American bishops mediated the dispute between growers and workers in 1970. Some conservative voices objected to the bishops' efforts, saying that they were favoring unionism. Cardinal Roger Mahoney of Los Angeles (then a priest and Auxiliary Bishop of Fresno) helped arrange talks between grape growers and the migrant workers that resulted in more equitable wages and contracts for the workers. The migrants' plight received national publicity and became a cause for many justice-minded Americans. In Chicago the bishops created a National Office for Catholic Migrants in 1960.

By that time there were Spanish-speaking Catholic groups in 57 archdioceses and dioceses. The Cursillo movement, a Latin-culture oriented retreat program, offered a Catholic spiritual experience to which the Hispanic community could relate. The bishops mixed the quest for political and economic independence with attempts to attract this population to the Catholic Church.

The 1950s and '60s brought Cuban refugees to the United States literally by the boatload, with thousands arriving monthly at the height of the exodus from Cuba. Miami served as the port of entry, and for tens of thousands of Cuban refugees, the final destination. Many received resettlement assistance from Catholic Relief Services. Many of these immigrants were well educated, successful, and anxious to keep their language and culture. Puerto Ricans gravitated north to New York City. An economic division arose among Spanish-speaking immigrants—some acquiring education, status and professions, others in the labor class struggling to make ends meet.

By 1964 there were an estimated 10 million Spanish-speaking residents in America (one-fifth of all Catholics in the country) coming from various Latin cultures.

Speaking Their Language

One of the difficulties in reaching the Hispanic population in America rested with the liturgy—conducted in Latin before Vatican II and in English after (for more on Vatican II, an important international meet-

A LEADER IN THE FIELDS

Some courageous visionaries did join the effort to help migrant workers. Caesar Chavez (1927–1993), the great Mexican-American social activist, attracted a great deal of attention to the migrant population not only in California but also all over the country.

Chavez was born in Arizona and became a labor organizer when he founded what became the United Farm Workers in 1962. His methods of nonviolent resistance to authority were modeled on Mohandas Gandhi (1869–1948), the renown Indian independence leader, as well as Saint Francis, a famous 12th century Catholic saint from Italy. Several times Chavez went on long fasts (spending long periods without eating). He moved beyond labor issues to become a major civil rights leader.

ing of Catholic bishops from 1962 to 1965, see page 44). The bishops recognized the need to develop a ritual in Spanish that would be understood by this community. Latin American bishops already had one, which the Americans adapted for their use.

Today the Hispanic Catholic population continues to grow although there is still significant movement to Protestant churches. The church tries to address the needs of the Spanish-speaking communities, but with only moderate success. When one pastor realized that the Spanish-speaking Catholics in Miami were reluctant to attend the main church, he set up several storefront churches as missions. These attracted large numbers, perhaps because the community was more comfortable with church services like those Evangelical Christians had popularized.

Many in the growing Latino/Latina population prefer to preserve their cultural heritage and language, insisting that the church attend to

On the picket lines
Cesar Chavez (center) is shown at the head of one of the many protest marches he led to publicize the cause of migrant workers. His campaign to get Americans to stop eating grapes helped gain recognition for the migrant worker issue.

their spiritual needs in ways that demonstrate sensitivity to and respect for their heritage. They do not wish to be forced into an "American" Catholicism that is dominated by European cultures. They claim that it is about time that the Church in America recognized their particular talents, growing numbers, and unique contributions without insisting that they take on the linguistic, religious, and social forms of the majority.

African-American Catholics

While the church attempted to nurture its ties with the Hispanic population, the church and society continued to struggle with their relationships to the black community. As African-Americans moved north in greater numbers to the burgeoning cities during the first half of the 20th century, they often encountered prejudice, bigotry, and hatred—from the pastor to the people in the pews. For example, at Holy Angels Parish in Chicago the pastor routinely requested his few African-American parishioners to sit in six back pews on the right side "and let the white people who built this church sit in the center." As late as the early 1950s, at Holy Name Church in Kansas City, a sign in front of the church urged blacks to attend Mass at a neighboring parish—until Rev. William R. Baron, OP, tore down the sign and invited all to participate in services.

The situation affected a number of closely held traditions. Neighborhoods of ethnic clans populated northern cities. German immigrants lived in "the German neighborhood" and worshiped at the German parish where the services were conducted in Latin (as they were in all Catholic churches), but the sermons were delivered in German and the parish conducted business in German. The same held true for the Polish, Italians, French, and so on. The Irish dominated the regular parishes.

African-Americans who migrated north looking for work in the factories and industries found themselves outsiders and unwelcome. Many parishioners feared that an encroaching black population would change the character of their neighborhoods and, as many argued, lower the value of their homes. Many white Catholics rationalized that segregation of races was natural and people wanted only to associate with their own race. The Catholic community ignored morality and enforced the segregation laws.

In this situation the Vatican led the way morally while many American Catholics perpetuated the sin of racism. On a number of occasions, the pope or Vatican officials expressed concern for the African-American community. After terrifying race riots in Chicago in 1919, the Vatican condemned the violence and urged bishops to address the issues of the black community. At that time only 2 percent of African-Americans were Catholic.

The Vatican's admonitions meant one thing; life in the neighborhoods and parishes meant another. Some sectors of the Catholic hierarchy acted responsibly, but others ignored Vatican warnings. Cardinal Francis Spellman opened all Catholic schools in New York to qualified African-American students in 1939, and the Jesuits began admitting black seminarians in 1945, as did St. Louis University. Others, however, including bishops and pastors, ignored Rome's urgings.

In 1958, the American bishops wrote a letter, "Discrimination and the Christian Conscience," which denounced segregation. However, it did not stem the tide of racism in the country or among Catholics. To accomplish that would take marches and civil disobedience, not pronouncements. It would take the 1960s and figures such as Martin Luther King, Jr., to energize churches to fight racism and alter the moral disposition of the United States.

Sticking With It

In a 1975 speech in Minneapolis, Brother Joseph M. Davis, then the director of the National Office for Black Catholics, said:

> [F]rom the beginning of the Catholic Church in America until the present day, Black Catholics have always felt as though they were marginal members of the Church, the step-children so to speak, the objects of the Church's missionary work, its outlet for charity.
>
> Because this may sound like a harsh indictment, we could miss altogether the truly tragic element that it contains. [That is] that for two centuries, despite what they have regarded as less than adequate, human, or [fair] treatment within the Church itself, Black Catholics have held their faith in the Church . . . . [They have] continued to push for full inclusion, believing that the Church must one day respond. The presence of black people in the American Catholic Church is nothing less than a living witness of faith, a continual call to justice within the Church.

In the 1960s, Americans confronted racism directly—sometimes violently, often nonviolently. Neighborhoods changed. African-Americans moved into the cities in increasing numbers, and whites fled to the rapidly growing suburbs. The term "inner-city" became part of the American vocabulary. In popular consciousness it signified poor, minority, run-down, and dangerous, with few opportunities. For the African-American population it signified all of these too; but it also meant home, their neighborhood. It meant families, churches, stores, schools, and playgrounds.

The style of worship in both Protestantism and Roman Catholicism appears stilted to the eyes and ears of many African-Americans. Protestantism denied them saints and sacred objects, and Catholicism offered little leeway in its liturgy for African expression via dance, song, or participation. In a 1986 article in *The Journal of the Interdenominational Theological Center*, black Catholic theologian Diana Hayes notes that contemporary black Catholics "see a structure which has tolerated their presence but not encouraged it. They see a structure which has required that they give up much of what was naturally theirs in order to become a part of an oppressive system in which many have never felt at home." Today only about 5 percent of American blacks are

Catholic, less than 3 percent of the church. There are fewer than 400 black priests in America, only a handful of whom are bishops.

Racism remains a problem to this day. Racist laws were ended but that has not eliminated racism in America or in some churches. As recently as 1997, the Louisiana bishops felt compelled yet again to dispel racist notions in a special letter to their people. Despite these attitudes among some, many black Catholics are loyal to the church, participate in parishes, and contribute richly to the Catholic community.

In the summer of 1997, cardinals, bishops, priests and laity participated in the dedication of Our Mother of Africa Chapel within the Basilica of the National Shrine of the Immaculate Conception in Washington, D.C., symbolizing a formal national recognition of black Catholics. In 2001, America's Catholic bishops elected Bishop Wilton Gregory, an African American, president of the United States Catholic Conference of Bishops.

City Parishes—and Parishioners—Change

The changing nature of urban neighborhoods had a huge impact on city parishes, most of which had been built during the heyday of immigrant Catholicism. Large complexes with a convent, school, rectory and church occupied an entire city block. They were a significant presence in the neighborhood. In the 1940s and '50s, real estate advertisements mentioned in what parish a house was located. The reputation and stability of the parish became a selling point. The residents themselves described where they lived by parish name and not street name or neighborhood. In many cases the population of sections of a city was overwhelmingly Catholic, so that Jews and Protestants found themselves outsiders in their own neighborhoods. Gradually, African-Americans moved in, replacing the Polish, Irish, and Italian Americans; the vast majority of these new residents were not Catholic.

This shift in population began a major social change. For decades Catholics had the run of the neighborhoods. Feast days were celebrated publicly, with streets blocked off to accommodate long processions of priests, nuns, and parishioners. May processions, filled with hundreds of girls in white dresses and boys in school uniforms, were annual springtime events that bestowed an identity on the neighborhood. For Corpus Christi processions (parades through the streets on the feast of the Body and Blood of Christ also celebrated in the spring), police and fire departments closed off sections of the neighborhood and set up temporary wooden structures, which served as altars. Parishioners scrubbed porches, steps, curbs, and streets in preparation for the special services that would take place. Flowers, ribbons, and banners filled the area, and people talked about the event all summer. These celebrations made up a part of the rhythm of the neighborhood.

The parish school was *the* school. Sports teams, socials, dances, funerals, missions, weddings, Lent (preceding Easter) and Advent (before Christmas) set the calendar and created a place in which people found a common identity. People walked to church. Children walked to the parish school, came home for lunch, went to Mass as a group, and wore uniforms, as had their brothers and sisters before them in the school. There was continuity and constant togetherness.

There was also fear of strangers. Catholics were told that they must not enter a Protestant church or a Jewish synagogue. Mixed marriages (between a Catholic and a non-Catholic) were discouraged, though not forbidden. Catholics who did choose to marry Protestants were not permitted to be married in the sanctuary of the church. They were relegated to the rectory in a quiet and brief ceremony or were allowed to have a ceremony outside of the altar rail in the church. Those who wished to marry non-Christians had an even more difficult task. Children born of a Protestant parent and a Catholic parent were said to be "the product" of a mixed marriage. In any case, the church ensured that the children would be brought up Catholic by requiring the non-Catholic party to sign a document promising to do so. Life for Catholics in America was like living on an all-Catholic island.

Asian Immigrants

Another important immigrant community that affected this sense of Catholic separation is the Asian community. Countries such as the Philippines, Korea, and Vietnam have nurtured Catholicism for centuries. When people from these and other Asian countries immigrate to the United States, they bring their Catholicism with them. Not unlike the Hispanic community, they bring with them certain customs and preferences that enrich the church in America.

Vietnamese Catholics strongly support the church. This community has yielded many students for the priesthood at a time when the church has a great need for clergy. Many of them arrived in Amer-

---

STILL GROWING

This chart shows from the National Catholic Directory shows the growth in the number of American Catholic parishes since World War II.

Year	Approx. # Parishes
1945	14,000
1955	16,000
1965	17,500
1975	18,200
1985	18,500
2000	18,750

ica as refugees during and after the Vietnam conflict in the 1960s and 1970s. Some were "boat people" who fled the Communist takeover of Vietnam with little more than the clothes on their backs. Vietnam has a long tradition of Catholicism and many American parishes welcomed them warmly. In some parishes today, Mass is celebrated in their native tongue. In others, they integrated with the existing community.

The Philippines also is home to many Catholics. Those who have immigrated to the United States maintain their ties to Catholicism and many have taken up roles as active members of their parishes. Filipino Catholics enrich the church with their cultural heritage as well.

Some Asians who came as refugees to America, for example the Hmongs from Cambodia and Thailand, had little knowledge of the country or Catholicism but the Church has welcomed them and assisted them to understand American culture. Some have become Catholics while others retain their native religion, but many have found a welcoming hand from the Church.

Coming of Age

While the Catholic Church continues to count immigrants among its number, most Catholics have been in America for several generations. In the 20th century Catholics came of age. They overcame obstacles, began to be accepted, and took advantage of opportunities. American Catholics make up 23 percent of the population. Their family size is the national average, their median income is higher than average, and they progress further in education than the average citizen. They occupy positions of power in all areas of the public and private sector.

They no longer are found only in certain regions of the country though they remain concentrated in some areas (such as the Northeast) and are more sparsely distributed in others (such as the Carolinas). Looked at statistically, they resemble their Protestant counterparts. Many prominent figures in business, politics, education, and the arts are Catholic. Martin Sheen, star of the popular television show *The West Wing*, three justices on the United States Supreme Court (Anthony Kennedy, Antonin Scalia, and Clarence Thomas), and political commentators Cokie Roberts and Tim Russert are Catholic.

Today Catholics may seem indistinguishable in American society, yet they have only recently emerged from their cohesive subculture to take their places in a pluralistic America.

TOP 10 CATHOLIC STATES	
State	# of Catholics (Millions)
California	9.8
New York	7.4
Texas	5.0
Illinois	3.8
Pennsylvania	3.5
New Jersey	3.4
Massachusetts	2.9
Michigan	2.2
Ohio	2.1
Florida	2.1

Source: Official Catholic Directory, 2001

Important American Catholic Events

MANY VISITORS TO CALIFORNIA MAKE IT A POINT TO STOP AT ONE of the beautiful missions that dot the Pacific coast. A mission is a church set up by a priest in a place where there has never been a church before. In the 18th century, missionary priests established missions in America to convert the native population to Christianity. They formed perhaps the first major Catholic presence in North America. The majority of these missionaries were Spanish Franciscan priests, men who were part of a religious community that followed the lifestyle of the 12th century Italian saint, Francis of Assisi.

Much of California's history began with the Spanish Missions. The string of 21 missions along California's El Camino Real ("The Royal Highway") traces both Catholic and American history. The missions range 650 miles along the California coast and are located a day's walk from one another. They have distinctive similar designs with a church, a bell tower, and a quadrangle for living and trade. Many California cities received their Spanish names from the missions, which were named after Catholic saints.

The first mission was started in 1769 by the Franciscan priest Father Junipero Serra at the direction of King Charles III of Spain. The king wanted to establish permanent settlements in California so that Spain could control the region, which he designated part of Spanish territory. The

Along the Mission Way

Here is a list of the missions started by Father Serra and his followers. All are now located in cities in California.

MISSION	YEAR	MISSION	YEAR
San Diego	1769	Santa Cruz	1791
San Carlos Borromeo (Carmel)	1770	Nuestra Senora de Soledad	1791
San Antonio de Padua	1771	San Jose	1797
San Gabriel	1771	San Juan Bautista	1797
San Luis Obispo	1772	San Miguel	1797
San Francisco de Asís	1776	San Fernando	1797
San Juan Capistrano	1776	San Luis Rey	1798
Santa Clara	1777	Santa Ines	1804
San Buenaventura	1782	San Rafael	1817
Santa Barbara	1786	San Francisco de Solano	1823
La Purisima Concepcion	1787		

PRECEDING PAGE
New World Catholics
The unique double bell tower of the Santa Barbara Mission watches over the Pacific Ocean high above the city. The mission was one of 21 founded by Franciscan priest Father Junipero Serra (1713–1784) of Spain. The settlements were among the first made by Catholic and European travelers in the Americas.

missionaries built near the coast where they could establish towns and trade with ships coming to port. Each church was built to be the height of the highest tree in the area so that it could be seen from a great distance.

The missionaries introduced Christianity to a region populated by Native Americans. Many historians today look upon the conversion of the Indians to Christianity as a less than honorable act in some ways. The missionaries forced the Indians to live in the missions, an unfamiliar habitat that proved to be unhealthy for the native population. The Spanish brought disease with them, to which the Native Americans had never been exposed. Many became ill and died. The Indians were forced to work on the mission farms raising wheat, corn, and grapes and caring for livestock. The missions grew what they needed, traded for other goods, and welcomed visitors. The Indians were virtually indentured servants that did the majority of the hard labor. However, they laid the early ground for a vibrant California economy.

Most of the Indians were baptized and became Christians. They took on the lifestyle and beliefs of the Spanish missionaries, even though both were foreign to them. However, by bringing so-called civilization to the Indians, the missionaries undermined the Native American civilization. Despite this unhappy legacy, the missionaries did develop California and left a heritage of missions that exist to this day.

St. Patrick's Cathedral in New York

A cathedral is the diocesan church presided over by the bishop. The most famous cathedral in America is Saint Patrick's Cathedral at 51st

A mighty building
Though dwarfed by nearby skyscrapers, St. Patrick's Cathedral remains a dominant force in American Catholic culture. This overhead view shows how the main body of a cathedral is laid out in the shape of a cross. St. Patrick's twin spires rise 330 feet above New York's Fifth Avenue.

Street and Fifth Avenue in New York City. This particular cathedral looms large (its spires climbing 330 feet) even in a city of skyscrapers. In 1853, Archbishop John Hughes chose the renowned architect James Renwick to design the cathedral of the Archdiocese of New York. Renwick, not a Catholic, came from a wealthy family that sent him to Columbia University in New York to study engineering. His architectural credits included Grace Church in New York, part of the Smithsonian Institution in Washington, D.C., and the New York Public Library. Archbishop Hughes wanted his cathedral to be a statement that Catholics had arrived and constituted a force in American society.

Hughes approached Renwick with the idea for the project and the engineer-turned-architect and his partner William Rodrique agreed to design the masterpiece. In 1858, Archbishop Hughes laid the cornerstone in front of more than 100,000 people. St. Patrick's construction, interrupted by the Civil War, took until 1879 to complete at a cost of $1.9 million. Even then, it lacked its notable steeples, which were only completed in 1908. It remains the largest Catholic cathedral in the country.

Named for Ireland's patron saint, the present cathedral replaced St. Patrick's Old Cathedral. That building had come under attack by an anti-Catholic and anti-immigrant mob in 1835. The archbishop called on a group of Irish-Catholics known as the Ancient Order of Hibernians to surround the cathedral walls to thwart the attack. Hughes warned the city's mayor that the Catholics would fight back. But a mob shouting "Paddies of the Pope" managed to stone the stained-glass windows of the Old Cathedral. The Old Cathedral survived the onslaught and now serves as a parish church. Since its construction, the new cathedral has come to symbolize Catholicism in America.

A National Voice

During World War I, American Catholics supported the war effort both by signing up to go to war and by caring for the troops in uniform. At the same time, American bishops created an organization called the National Catholic War Council that promoted conversation among the bishops and gave them a way to speak with one voice to the American people, both Catholics and non-Catholics alike. This new national organization also tried to influence American public policy by speaking directly to politicians in both parties.

At first the Vatican did not favor the creation of such a body, since Rome was accustomed to making policy for the international church. It did not relish the idea of an independent American body speaking for the church. However, the pope was persuaded to endorse the organization and the American bishops had their method to speak to Catholics and to address issues that affected American society at large.

This organization gave the American bishops one voice on national matters. After World War I, they changed the name of the organization to the National Catholic Welfare Conference, a name that remained until 1966, when it was changed again to the National Conference of Catholic Bishops. Since 2001 it has been called the United States Conference of Catholic Bishops (USCCB) and is based in Washington, D.C. The USCCB includes offices that work on many different aspects of the Church's mission. The bishops work with other Catholics to address issues that concern the Church as part of the larger society.

The bishops' concerns range from African-American Catholics to World Missions. Two of the departments directly related to the United States are the Government Liaison Department and the Faithful Citizen Department. The first monitors Congress and lobbies for legislation favorable to the church's positions. The second helps instruct Catholics on how to be responsible participants in the civic order, specifically as Catholics. This department informs Catholics of the moral dimensions of public policies and urges them to vote the basis of Catholic principles.

Their statement of goals reads in part, "As Catholics we need to share our values, raise our voices, and use our votes to shape a society that protects human life, promotes family life, pursues social justice, and practices solidarity." While they do not advise Catholics for whom they should vote, they do inform them of Catholic social teachings in the hope that American parishioners will support the candidates who agree with the church's positions.

The creation of a body that represents American Catholics in many areas increased the Church's visibility in the country. Ordinary Catholics may not all think alike, and they sometimes disagree with the bishops, but they understand the value of having a unified organization. Those in power in the United States cannot ignore a highly structured church.

The G. I. Bill

In the 1950s Catholics were working their way up the social ladder in America and at the same time were very loyal to Rome. Two developments changed the way American Catholics acted. The first was World War II, and the second was the G. I. Bill. Catholics signed up in large numbers to serve in the military during World War II. Catholics generally have been good citizens, loyal to both their country and their Church. When the soldiers returned from the war, the government gave them benefits specified in the so-called G.I. Bill that helped to pay for college tuition. With these benefits, many Catholics (and others) who previously could not have afforded college now could enroll, and enroll they did in record numbers. Equipped with better educations, they could enter the professions, secure well-paying jobs, and take leadership roles in business, government, education, and other fields. Many private universities, previously off limits to Catholics, began to admit them in significant numbers. Corporations hired them and the professions welcomed them. Finally, they had overcome discrimination and began to make their mark in society

Access to higher education enabled American Catholics to compete equally with others in America and to begin to move up the corporate ladder in business and the professions. This led to an increased expectation for education among the baby-boomer generation (those born between 1946 and 1964). At the same time that they were pursuing college degrees, the society was becoming more accepting of Catholics. Catholics began to have careers in business, politics, higher education, medicine, law and other professions. They started in entry-level positions and for awhile were confined to middle management positions, but eventually many worked their way to the top. .

One of the unintended consequences of this rise was that Catholics no longer looked different from others in America and they began to adopt ways of thinking and doing that reflected American culture more than Catholic teaching. In some ways they became more mainstream American but less Catholic.

The Second Vatican Council

Another major event that dramatically changed American Catholics (and Catholics all over the world) was the Second Vatican Council (known as Vatican II), held at the Vatican in Rome from 1962 to 1965.

The council, a meeting of the leaders from the universal church, set an agenda for the church in the modern world. No longer would the church stubbornly resist contemporary culture; in fact, now it would embrace much of it.

The council was called by Pope John XXIII, who, elected pope at 77 years old, was not expected to change the church. He surprised most observers when he called more than 2,600 bishops, along with theologians and observers from other Christian churches, to the Vatican for a meeting that would set a course for the church in the future. He used an Italian word, *aggiornamento*, to describe the mission of the council. The word means "to open the windows," to let a fresh breeze blow the cobwebs out of the church. It also signaled the opening of the church to the world. The fact that bishops came to the council from all corners of the world confirmed that this was truly a world church. For a long time European bishops dominated the church, but this council gave voice to the Third World and to Americans as never before. The council participants described the church as "the People of God," meaning that the church represents everyone in it, not just bishops and priests.

Vatican II issued 16 documents designed to direct the Church toward its future. When the church began to put into practice the advice from these documents, many things changed—from the language of the Mass (in America, from Latin to English) to more contemporary clothing worn by nuns.

Before Vatican II, Catholic Mass was conducted in the ancient language of Latin, giving it a certain mysterious character. However, the vast majority of Catholics did not understand Latin, and they acted more as observers of the Mass than as participants. Vatican II changed the language of the Mass to the vernacular (the language used by the people of a country) and invited Catholics to participate by responding to prayers, distributing communion, and singing contemporary liturgical songs. Before Vatican II Catholics received communion on their tongues while kneeling at an altar rail. Catholics now receive communion in their hands while standing.

As everywhere else worldwide, the council profoundly affected the church in America. Ordinary Catholics now enjoyed greater authority in the parish as Parish Councils were established, composed of people who attended Mass there. These councils advise pastors on a wide range of issues affecting their local church. New, upbeat music and modern instruments (often guitars) replaced or joined with traditional organ music at church services.

After Vatican II churches were redesigned, moving the altar closer to the congregation with the priest facing the people instead of with his back to them as in the pre-Vatican II liturgy. For some Catholics these changes came too quickly, resulting in resentment or disenchantment. They felt that the church they had known all their lives had begun to slip away. The transition proved difficult for them, as well as for some priests. Others, however, welcomed the changes as long over-

THE OLD WAY

Here are some of the Latin phrases used in the Catholic Mass before Vatican II. Older Catholic Americans remember these as part of their childhood.

Intro ibo ad altare Dei
I go before the altar of God

Pax vobiscum
Peace be with you

Et cum spirtu tuo
And also with you

In nomini Patri, Filii, et Spiritu Sanctu
In the name of the Father, Son, and Holy Spirit

Oremus
Let us pray

Agnus dei
Lamb of God

Requiescat in pace
Rest in peace (used at funerals)

due. The years immediately following the council were filled with change but were exciting. The church enjoyed a new vibrancy and the Catholic people claimed a voice in the church.

Change occurred at a different pace depending upon the local bishop and the local pastor. Many parishes experimented with different styles of liturgy including homilies (sermons) that were more of a conversation than a speech. They invited lay people to participate in ministry and began to include women in the decision-making process.

The church after Vatican II experienced a split between conservatives and liberals. Some conservatives wanted to return to pre-Vatican II practices such as the Latin Mass while liberals wanted to implement changes more quickly. The church continues to deal with the effects of Vatican II even today.

A Catholic President

In many towns and cities in the United States, Catholics played key roles in local politics. Nevertheless, they lacked influence in national politics. In 1928 when the Democrats nominated the popular New York governor Al Smith as their candidate for president, many voters harbored prejudice against him because he was a Catholic. They feared that a Catholic in the White House would listen to the pope as much as to the American people. Many felt that Catholics' loyalty to the pope interfered with their American citizenship. They did not like the idea of a "foreign power" possibly intervening in American politics and government. Anti-Catholic sentiment helped to defeat Smith in the election. (After the election a story circulated that after losing, Governor Smith sent the pope a one-word message: "Unpack.")

Political experts knew the pope would not be involved in American policy, but many regular voters had deep suspicions about Catholics in general, and Catholic politicians in particular. They were not about to give them the opportunity to demonstrate their loyalty to their country by electing one president of the United States.

This prejudice lasted for another 32 years. In 1960, John F. Kennedy, a senator from Massachusetts, won the nomination of the Democratic party to run for the presidency. Kennedy, an Irish Catholic, came from a very prominent family that enjoyed both wealth and political success. He had been educated in fine schools not normally friendly to Catholics. However, because of his family's prominence and his own intelligence, Kennedy was able to move in circles usually off-limits to Catholics. Nevertheless, his Catholicism proved to be a hurdle in the election. Shadows of the prejudice that Smith encountered in the 1920s still lingered in the late 1950s. It did not matter whether Kennedy observed all of the rules of Catholicism—and in fact, he did not observe all of them. The fact that he was a Catholic counted against him in some quarters.

Thus he faced a dilemma in his campaign. Should he distance himself from his religion, and if so, how could he do it without offending Catholics? He was not about to renounce his religion, but he knew that he had to reassure the American public that he would not be a puppet for the pope. It required a delicate balance of patriotism and faith. He had been campaigning for months but the questions about his Catholicism could not be quieted. He needed to confront the issue head on and either explain his relationship to Catholicism to the voter's satisfaction or perhaps suffer the same fate as Al Smith. He was in a very tight race with a skilled political opponent, Richard Nixon.

In the final months before the election, with the campaign heating up, Kennedy found his opportunity to address the issue. The Greater Houston Ministerial Association, a group of 300 evangelical Protestant clergymen, invited Kennedy to address them on September 12, 1960. This gave him an opportunity to clear the air about the role his religion might or might not play in his presidency. He expressed his views on the relation between religion and politics. He pointed to the fact that in his political career thus far, he had always respected the separation of church and state and indicated that he intended to maintain that disposition during his presidency if elected. He insisted that the president and the country must be governed by its Constitution and laws, not by religious oaths.

Kennedy's strategy worked. In a very close election in November 1960, he defeated Nixon and assumed office as the 35th president of the United States on January 20, 1961. Historians and political scientists view his election as both an end and a beginning. It ended, for the most part, anti-Catholic sentiment in the country, especially since Kennedy went on to become a popular president and did not interject his religious beliefs into his executive decisions.

It began an era in American politics in which religion and governing remain firmly separated. In 2001, President George W. Bush's

AN IMPORTANT SPEECH

Here is a short excerpt from John Kennedy's important 1960 campaign speech to ministers in Houston:

I am not the Catholic candidate for president. I am the Democratic Party's candidate for president, who happens also to be a Catholic.

Whatever issues come before me as president, if I should be elected—on birth control, divorce, censorship, or any other subject—I will make my decision in accordance . . . with what my conscience tells me to be in the national interest, and without regard to outside religious pressure or dictate.

Pope on the road
Pope John Paul II's many visits to the United States have helped focus attention on the nation's Catholic population. His visibility has helped raise the profile of the American Catholic Church as well. Here he meets with President Ronald Reagan in 1984.

efforts for faith-based initiatives funded by the government encountered resistance because Americans remain wary when religion and politics mix. Also, since Kennedy's election, the Catholicism of elected officials appears not to affect voters negatively as it used to. Roman Catholics now regularly make up the largest single religious denomination in the United States Congress.

Pope John Paul II Visits America

No pope has traveled as much as John Paul II, who became pope in 1978. He visited the United States seven times during his papacy (1979, 1980, 1984, 1987, 1993, 1995, and 1999). A charismatic figure, on each visit the pope achieved celebrity status usually reserved for rock stars. In 1994, *Time* magazine named him the "Man of the Year". Every American, whether Catholic or even a believer, knows the pope. He is a spiritual leader, a head of state, and an international celebrity. On his visits to the United States, huge crowds of people lined the streets to get a glimpse of him as he traveled in his custom "Popemobile." He addressed the

The Pope Speaks

In 1979, Pope John Paul II visited New York City. While there, he spoke to the United Nations General Assembly about the Church's views on many issues. His list of human rights had particular appeal in America, a nation founded based on such rights. Here is a section of that speech:

> Permit me to [list] some of the most important human rights that are universally recognized: the right to life, liberty and security of person; the right to food, clothing, housing, sufficient health care, rest and leisure; the right to freedom of expression, education and culture; the right to [practice] one's religion either individually or in community, in public or in private; the right to choose a state of life, to found a family and to enjoy all conditions necessary for family life; the right to property and work, to adequate working conditions and a [fair] wage; the right of assembly and association; the right to freedom of movement, to internal and external migration; the right to nationality and residence; the right to political participation and the right to participate in the free choice of the political system of the people to which one belongs.

United Nations General Assembly twice (1979 and 1995), and celebrated Mass before hundreds of thousands in public venues such as Giants Stadium, New York's Central Park, and Baltimore's Camden Yards baseball stadiums.

The pope's many visits to the United States underscore the importance of American Catholics. As a developed and affluent nation, America holds an important position on the world stage and American Catholics have a responsibility to be an example of Christian charity and generosity to the world. Pope John Paul II, able to speak many languages, addressed the crowds in English and instructed them to follow the way of Jesus no matter what the cost. When the pope disagreed with American laws or social patterns, he forcefully spoke out against them, just as he has done in other countries he has visited. He has had meetings with many U.S. presidents to exchange views on pressing moral issues of the day.

The pope uses his popularity and notoriety to convey the message of the church to the world. Politically, his independence allows him to speak freely and forcefully about moral practices that he believes need to be upheld or, in some instances, corrected. Thus he publicly opposed American consumer culture, legal abortion, capital punishment, and the lure of the worldly over the holy. Of course, not every American agrees with him on all issues, not even Catholics, but he speaks with a clear voice, passion, and deep moral convictions. Americans may not always agree with him, but they regularly listen to him.

His visits excited not only Catholics but all Americans, many of whom wished to get a glance of him in person. Most other religions in the world do not have a single leader who commands the attention of the entire world. These visits raised the profile of American Catholics in their own country and were a source of pride for Catholics.

Catholic Impact on American Culture

AMERICAN CULTURE NOT ONLY INFLUENCES CATHOLICS, AS SEEN IN previous chapters, but Catholics also influence American culture. The 65 million American Catholics make a difference. In the course of its history in America, the church has established many structures that affect all Americans. These institutions often serve a population wider than just Catholics. Because of this, the Catholic Church touches the lives of many Americans.

Catholic Schools

Nowhere has the impact of Catholics on American culture been felt more greatly than through Catholic schools. From the elementary level to universities, Catholic schools have helped shape the lives of millions of Catholics and more recently, an increasing number of non-Catholics. One of the major reasons that Catholics developed such an extensive network of schools was the prejudice that Catholics experienced in early America. Unwelcome in private Protestant schools, Catholics needed to create their own system of education. Public schools were open to them, but these schools tended to favor Protestant ways of thinking, including the use of a Protestant Bible. So Catholic bishops and pastors decided to create a system in which Catholics would feel comfortable and which would teach Catholic doctrine.

Today, millions of school children attend these Catholic schools, which are found in every state. The alumni of these schools are even more numerous. Thus, many Catholics have an education that unites them with their church. These schools teach religious instruction as part of the curriculum, and they reinforce the values and teachings of the church. Many of these schools, especially at the elementary school level, are associated with parishes and can be found serving neighborhoods where the parishes are located. Catholic high schools often serve a broader geographical area, bringing teenagers from several parishes together. Catholic colleges and universities exist across the United States and enroll both Catholics and non-Catholics. Some well-known ones such as Georgetown, Notre Dame, and Boston College, include graduate programs and professional schools as well as undergraduate education.

Catholic schools grew at their fastest pace after the American bishops committed the church's resources and energy to them in a series of councils held in Baltimore in 1852, 1886, and 1884. The bishops recommended that every parish establish a school; many followed these instructions and built schools on parish property. The parishes recruited nuns to teach in the schools; tens of thousands of dedicated, hard-working sisters spent their lives teaching and forming the spiritual and moral character of hundreds of thousands of Catholic school children. Parishes kept tuition rates low so that immigrant families could afford to send their children. Sometimes large families would have three, four, or five children in a Catholic school. By the time the youngest child went through the school, the nuns knew all of his or her siblings and the parish priests knew the family well. This helped create stable and friendly Catholic communities. The Catholic influence extended beyond the school into the family. The church united families and gave the Catholic community identity and visibility.

Religious orders—large groups of sisters, brothers, or priests—played a key role in the development of Catholic education. Each religious order performed a particular type of ministry in the church depending upon the charisma (special talents) of its founder. Many orders of sisters were founded specifically to be involved with education. Also, orders of brothers, such as the Christian Brothers, and priests, such as the Jesuits, have dedicated much of their efforts to education. Many of these orders founded colleges and universities to meet the need for

higher education for Catholics. As a result, today hundreds of Catholic colleges and universities enroll a religiously diverse student body, educating them to be doctors, lawyers, engineers, teachers, business executives, and any number of other careers.

The number of nuns, priests, and brothers has declined in recent decades, so most personnel in Catholic schools are laypeople who continue the mission of Catholic education. They continue to teach the values of Catholicism and to carry on the important work of educating the next generation.

Catholics Go to the Movies

The Catholic bishops of the United States maintain a Web site (see page 123) that advises Catholics about which movies are wholesome and which are objectionable. Many younger Catholics are not aware of this, although their parents and grandparents remember a time when the church had a powerful influence over the movie-going habits of Catholics. In fact, its opinions actually influenced what films were made.

National Catholic officials have their own rating system for movies. It is different from the familiar G, PG, PG-13, and R ratings that all movies use (see box on page 55). It appears that only a small percentage of Catholics pay any attention to these ratings, since many of the movies that the church finds objectionable continue to draw large audiences—no doubt a significant portion of which are Catholics. Earlier, however, Catholic ratings as created by church officials were very important to the Catholic movie-going public.

Shortly after the introduction of sound to movies in the 1920s, the church began to call publicly for censorship of films. Influential American bishop John Cantwell of Los Angeles (the home of the movie industry) decided to do something, together with wealthy publisher Martin Quigley, Sr. They convinced the newly appointed Apostolic Delegate from the Vatican to the United States (a sort of ambassador) to criticize the motion picture industry in a 1933 speech.

In 1934 Cardinal Dennis Dougherty of Philadelphia took the drastic measure of forbidding Catholics in his archdiocese from going to the movies at all, saying that movie theaters constituted an "occasion [opportunity] of sin." Obedient Catholics followed the cardinal's rule. Some Protestants joined the protest, causing business to decline 40 percent and forcing some movie theaters to close. Even personal visits from movie industry executive Samuel Goldwyn could not persuade Dougherty to lift his prohibition.

Many bishops and priests were condemning the movie industry and objecting to individual films from their pulpits with significant results, as revenues for these films fell dramatically. The national bishops' committee formed the Legion of Decency and asked each Catholic to pledge an oath to avoid any movie deemed objectionable. On every December 8 for years, millions of Catholics took a version of this pledge during the Mass honoring Mary, the mother of Jesus. The Legion of Decency also established a rating system to grade films.

At about the same time, in response to potential censorship, the motion picture industry established its own Production Code Administration for self-regulation. This system had a significant impact on the industry. Producers and directors made sure that the films they created would meet these standards. Some projects were abandoned and others were edited to follow the rules.

While the Legion of Decency's pledge may strike a Catholic moviegoer today as an excessive form of censorship, it does find an echo in many people's dislike of the violence in films. Less disturbing to today's viewer is the treatment of sexual matters on screen. At the time of the Legion of Decency, objectionable matter included references to divorce, extramarital or premarital sex, exposure of a woman's legs, and even on-screen kisses longer than a few seconds.

The Movies React

The Production Code and the Legion of Decency maintained their combined moral authority over the movie industry into the 1950s. After much wrangling, some film makers and studios, such as United Artists, ignored the ratings system. European films, in which the standards of morality appeared looser, were also making their way into American theaters. Even though intense pressure was exerted on movie theaters not to show such films, profit motives and the preferences of the viewing public often won out. Post-World War II Americans wanted more realistic films. In 1956, the Production Code was loosened, and in 1959 the Legion of Decency's pledge was rewritten. In 1965 the Legion changed its name to the National Catholic Office for Motion Pictures. By 1970 parishes no longer led parishioners in the pledge.

The movie industry itself, however, introduced a new rating system in 1968, in response to the public's desire to know whether a film contained nudity, adult language, or violence. In 1997, after public pressure and congressional inquiries, the television industry followed suit with a voluntary rating system for television programs. One of the reasons for the new system was that in the 1990s television shows, particularly those shown after nine at night, had become more, not less, explicit. Warnings alert viewers to violence and adult language and situations.

The battle for moral control of the big screen continues today, even if the heyday of the church as a voice that receives a wide hearing is over. The church continues to be concerned about the influence of films on morality in an era when advocates of censorship have not been able to limit pornography on the Internet—a medium without the history of films, but an increasingly influential one.

Today film makers no longer stick to the rules that guided studios at least until the 1960s. In that era films were not allowed to ridicule faith, priests or ministers, and religious rituals commanded respect. Today the film and television industries are less concerned about offending religious sensibilities. The movie industry is much less

> **CATHOLIC MOVIE RATINGS**
>
> **A-I:** General Patronage (appropriate for all ages)
>
> **A-II:** Adults and teenagers
>
> **A-III:** Adults
>
> **A-IV:** Adults, with reservations; these films are not necessarily offensive, but viewers should proceed cautiously
>
> **O:** Morally offensive

sensitive to criticism from the church. Cultural freedom and independence have drowned out the church's objections to particular films. Movie studios no longer worry about movie ratings issued from the church since most Catholics themselves do not pay attention to them.

While the church may wish to censor films or the Internet, it cannot effectively do so. While it continues to offer advice on what is suitable for viewing by young people (or older people for that matter), its impact appears to be minimal on the views or Web-surfing habits of the American public, Catholics included.

A movie priest
Bing Crosby (center), a Catholic actor and singer, portrayed a priest in the movie Going My Way, *winning an Oscar in 1944 for his role in the popular film.*

"Catholic" Films

Because of fears that the church might object, *The Ten Commandments* is the last movie with a religious theme that some older Catholics have seen. Yet there have been other films of note that have had a Christian theme, if not specifically Catholic. In the 1960s, *Godspell* was a successful Broadway play and a movie that cast Jesus in the figure of a carefree clown. This was followed on stage and film by the very human characterization of Jesus in *Jesus Christ Superstar* in 1973. These two plays also had commercially successful soundtracks.

Franco Zeffirelli's *Jesus of Nazareth* (1978), filmed in Israel, attempted to be sensitive and true to the biblical story. Director Martin Scorcese adapted the novel *The Last Temptation of Christ* for the screen in 1988. The film included a controversial dream scene in which Jesus marries Mary Magdalene. Some Catholics staged protests against the movie outside theater entrances. Older Catholics remembered the days when the church would have simply banned Catholics from seeing the movie. However, by that time the idea of censorship was more offensive to more people than the way in which Jesus was depicted in this film.

In 1988, the film *Romero* chronicled the life and death by assassination of the El Salvador bishop and champion of human rights Oscar Romero. It was more of a celebration of Catholic life and the power of one man of faith. But its violent content in places also made it hard for Catholic officials to recommend it highly.

The 1995 film *The Priest* stirred the strongest reaction. The movie depicts a troubled priest and an uncaring bishop—hardly a positive image of men of the cloth. It is a far cry from the Bing Crosby films of the 1940s, such as *Going My Way* and *The Bells of St. Mary's*. Crosby, himself a Catholic, played priests as moral giants and gentle souls. *Going My Way* won the Oscar for best picture in 1944 and Crosby won the Oscar for best actor. *The Priest*, on the other hand, was gritty, realistic, and hotly debated in the press. Again, the issue of the church's role in trying to censor movies outweighed most consideration of the church's feelings about the movie. By the 1990s, it was almost becoming counterproductive for the church to speak out strongly against movies, television, or other popular entertainments. The ongoing debate was just part of the continuing collision of Catholic doctrine with American freedoms and opinions.

The Catholic Press

Since the advent of the printing press and the publication of the first Gutenberg Bibles, the church has had an interest in putting its message into print. The oldest Catholic newspaper in this country, *Le Propagateur Catholique*, was published in French in New Orleans in 1810. The pioneer Catholic newspaper in English, *United States Catholic Miscellany*, appeared in Charleston, South Carolina, in 1822. Today in America there is a vast publishing industry connected to Catholicism; some of it educates, some analyzes, some proselytizes, and some criticizes.

At the local level, every diocese in America has its own newspaper. These papers usually are weeklies designed to keep the local Catholic population informed. They regularly cover news from the Vatican, publish official church statements from Rome and the National Conference of Catholic Bishops, report national news that relates to Catholics or issues of concern to Catholics, and perhaps most important, act as a voice for the local bishop and diocese. These papers generally avoid controversial reporting and print only those stories that are consistent with church policy. Some of these diocesan papers carry syndicated columns written by theologians, clergy, or laypersons. The subject of these articles is, therefore, not under the control of the local editor, and occasionally controversial subjects are covered in these articles. Sometimes these papers are interested in how events affect Catholics only, with headlines such as "Six People Die in Crash, Two Catholic." This narrow view has its counterpart in the nonreligious press when a story with an international scope identifies only the Americans involved.

To support the Catholic press, some dioceses circulate their papers through the parishes, either by distributing them after Masses in the foyer of the church or having them sent directly to registered parishioners and billing the parish for the cost.

In addition to local newspapers, there are a few national Catholic newspapers. Two of the best known are the *Wanderer*, favored by conservatives, and the *National Catholic Reporter* (*NCR*), which takes a liberal position on most issues. These weeklies are mailed to subscribers. *NCR* began in October 1964 in response to the Second Vatican Council. It is an independent paper published in Kansas City, Missouri, by laypeople. The paper also maintains a Web site (see page 123). The same organization publishes Sheed & Ward books, Credence Cassettes, the liturgical magazine *Celebration*, and the magazine *Praying*. *The Wanderer*, begun in 1867, has a circulation of approximately 37,000, while the *NCR*'s circulation is about 50,000, small numbers when considering that there are 65 million Catholics in America today.

Catholic weekly magazines reach a wider number of readers, Catholic and non-Catholic alike, and are often quoted in national discussions about Catholic issues. *Commonweal* and *America* tend toward the liberal side, while *Crisis* and *Our Sunday Visitor* lean toward the conservative. *Commonweal* is edited by Catholic lay people, and *America* is a Jesuit publication. As in the case of the movies, American Catholics have become much more diverse in their search for news and opinions and do not depend on the Catholic view. Non-Catholics, meanwhile, consult such magazines for a look inside the current state of Catholic thought and debate.

As for books, the Catholic book industry is extensive and diverse, publishing everything from Bibles to textbooks. A large commercial interest in religious education is served by publishers such as Sadlier and Silver Burdett. Catholic theologians are not forced to publish their work with Catholic presses, and many prominent theologians use secular or traditionally Protestant publishing houses. However, a number of Catholic presses are dedicated to theology and spirituality, such as Paulist, Orbis, and Sheed & Ward. These are complemented by university presses such as those of the Catholic University of America and Georgetown University, which publish works primarily for scholars.

The church exerts some control over the content of Catholic books by granting its permission to publish those books that it approves (the official name for this permission is a term from Latin, *imprimatur*), meaning that they contain nothing against the faith and are unlikely to be incorrect spiritually. In addition, the church indicates that such a book is free from doctrinal error by giving it a *nihil obstat* (the Latin term for "nothing objectionable"), though this does not constitute an endorsement of the book. A bishop grants the *imprimatur,* and the *nihil obstat* is given by a theologian charged by the bishop with that responsibility. Usually the church grants the *imprimatur* to a small range of books like Bibles and liturgical texts, textbooks for religious education, and books displayed or sold in churches. However, most books published by Catholic presses do not ask for or receive these special approvals.

CATHOLIC NEWS SERVICE

Much of the material published in national and local Catholic newspapers originates from the Catholic News Service (CNS), America's oldest and largest news wire service. Both print and broadcast media (including Vatican Radio) rely on CNS for stories about Catholicism and reports on issues relating to Catholics.

CNS was created by the U.S. bishops in 1920 and operates under the jurisdiction of the USCCB but maintains editorial and financial independence. In addition to its own team of reporters, CNS maintains ties with other news organizations in order to cover the world as accurately and fully as possible.

Television

The church has not ignored the opportunity to communicate its message on television. Alongside the names of famous Protestant preachers Billy Graham and Robert Schuller stand Catholics Bishop Fulton J. Sheen and Mother Angelica.

In the 1930s, Sheen, a priest from Peoria, Illinois, became a weekly guest in the home of millions of Catholics and others on his radio show *The Catholic Hour*. From 1951 to 1957 he had a television show called *Life is Worth Living*, and in 1966 another one called *The Bishop Sheen Program* (he was named Auxiliary Bishop of the Archdiocese of New York, in 1951 and Bishop of Rochester, New York, in 1966). A spellbinding preacher, Sheen was the public face of Catholicism to a generation of Catholics and non-Catholics alike.

In 1981 Eternal Word Television Network began on cable television. Since then, EWTN has grown into the largest religious cable network, broadcasting to over 55 million homes in 38 countries. The charismatic figure of the network is Mother Angelica, through her show *Mother Angelica Live*. In addition, programming includes a teaching series on Catholicism called *Pillars of Faith*, and a teen-young adult segment called *Life on the Rock*. The network, and Mother Angelica in particular, has used the medium of cable television effectively. Her traditional views, coupled with her occasional criticism of the positions of some bishops, means that her show appeals mostly to a conservative segment of the Catholic population.

Radio

Despite the popularity of television and the information revolution brought about by the computer, radio remains an important medium of communication for the church. In the heyday of radio during the 1930s and 1940s, the church's best known voice was that of Father Charles E. Coughlin, a pastor from Royal Oak, Michigan, who attracted an audience of millions with his Sunday radio broadcasts. Coughlin did not shy away from political affairs. Nor was he afraid to change his mind and the minds of his listeners. In the 1930s, at the beginning of the presidency of Franklin D. Roosevelt, he was a strong supporter of the New Deal. Over time he retreated from Roosevelt and saw the New Deal as a raw deal for Americans. He became increasingly fearful of Communism, criticized Jews, and became sympathetic to Adolf

She wants her nun TV
Mother Angelica's talk shows and lectures are among the most popular programs on the Catholic-themed EWTN. She mixes old-fashioned values with a modern approach to television.

Hitler in the years before World War II. His inflammatory speeches drew so much attention to the church that Cardinal George Mundelein of Chicago stepped in to denounce Coughlin's message. Shortly after America's entrance into the war, Coughlin left the air.

Today, with VCRs, DVDs, satellite TV, and cable, radio is no longer the dominant medium that it was in the 1930s. The Catholic presence on radio has not disappeared, however. In March 1996 the Eternal Word Television Network began broadcasting radio shows in English and Spanish to AM and FM stations around the world via satellite. Programming includes a news service that keeps Catholics informed of the pope's statements and stories of interest to Catholics.

An organization called UndaUSA (*Unda* is Latin for "wave"), part of UndaWorld, the International Catholic Association for Radio and Television, opened national offices in 1972 in Dayton, Ohio. UndaUSA brings together media professionals who want to further the mission of the church through electronic media. The Catholic Broadcasters Association seeks to bring the gospel to Americans via the airwaves.

All of these media ventures by the church result in Catholics being informed about the official church's positions on a wide range of issues. The Church has a presence in the established media, and it is increasingly moving into the electronic media to get its message across, in particular on the Web.

Catholicism on the Web

Today the universal church, and the American church in particular, is connected to and invested in modern communications technology. If you surf the Internet looking for Catholic sites, you will find how committed the church is to getting its message across electronically. From the Vatican to the United States Conference of Catholic Bishops, Catholics now have electronic access to a wealth of information from and about the church. For example, Catholic Online attempts to fulfill the pope's wishes for instant access to information and for loyalty by assuring those who log-on that they are loyal to the pope and faithful to the church.

The Vatican Web page (see page 123), available in six languages (English, Dutch, French, Spanish, Italian, and Portuguese), posts important papal documents and news, and has an on-line tour of the Vatican Museum. The site includes a biography of Pope John Paul II, lists

www.vatican.va
Coming a long way from ancient scrolls and hand-printed Bibles, today's Catholic Church spreads the word about its mission and its beliefs via Web sites such as the one operated by the Vatican, worldwide center of the church.

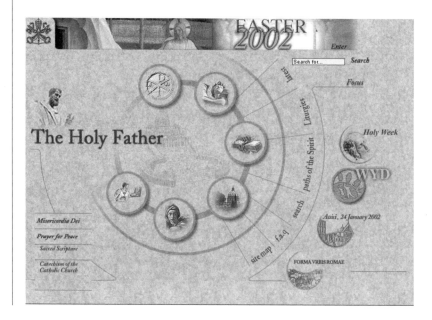

of prayers, and provides information about official Catholic teachings and beliefs.

The proliferation of Catholic Web sites has some church officials worried. In February 1997, Cardinal Roger Mahoney of Los Angeles voiced his concern to the Pontifical Council for Social Communications at the Vatican. "There are too many 'Catholic [Web] sites and services that are questionable," he wrote. "The church needs to take immediate steps to authorize and authenticate electronic services that utilize the name 'Catholic,' while disallowing those that are illegitimate and so informing unsuspecting users."

In 2002, the Vatican issued two documents that addressed the use of the Internet. The first reflected some of the church's concerns about the use and potential abuse of this medium. The second assessed the ways the Internet could help parishes. Also, the church wants to ensure that the Internet does not divide people between the "haves" and the "have nots." It urges societies, companies, and governments to do everything possible to provide equal access to this powerful tool, to avoid a digital divide that supplies the wealthy with valuable information and leaves the poor ignorant. It also encourages those who furnish content and technology for the Internet to do so in several languages so that non-English speakers are not left on the sidelines. The second document emphasized how valuable the Internet can be for communicating the Church's message to young people who turn to the Internet as a key source of information.

Computers also provide new avenues for connection to the Church. The American bishops, most dioceses, and many parishes have Web sites by which they can provide information, invite interaction, and extend the church's reach into the home and workplace in new ways. The church's considerable collection of art is accessible via computer, and Rome can communicate its message worldwide without delay and without the pope having to leave the Vatican.

Religious education programs can be on-line, parish registration can take place online, and parish committee news can be posted on the Web as parishes now post copies of their weekly bulletin. While none of this is the same as personal contact, and the church is not about to become a virtual community, it does speed communication and provide more ready access to information. In tradition-laden Catholicism, it is a brave new world.

THE POPE ON THE INTERNET

In a document tilted *The Church and Computer Culture*, published in 1989, Pope John Paul II wrote:

With the advent of computer telecommunications and computer participation systems, the Church is offered further means for fulfilling her mission. Methods of [easing] communication and dialogue among her own members can strengthen the bonds of unity between them. Immediate access to information makes it possible for her to deepen her dialogue with the contemporary world. In the new "computer culture," the Church can more readily inform the world of her beliefs and explain the reasons for her stance on any given issue or event.

Literature

The literary world in America has always been dominated by writers from a Protestant background. Even as recently as the late 1800s, early American Puritanism was still being wrestled with in the novels of Nathaniel Hawthorne and the stories of Mary Wilkins Freeman—both descendants of American Puritans. In the 20th century, Catholic writers began to lay claim to their own corner of the literary world.

From the beginning of the last century, as greater numbers of European Catholic immigrants poured into the country, Catholics could boast at least one prominent writer in every literary generation. Though many—such as Kate Chopin, F. Scott Fitzgerald, and Jack Kerouac—were more Catholic by birth than practice, others consciously worked at creating a Catholic identity. Among these were Flannery O'Connor and Walker Percy (a convert to Catholicism), both Southerners writing in the middle part of the century. In novels like O'Connor's *The Violent Bear It Away* and Percy's *The Moviegoer*, characters live lives in search of grace and salvation in a difficult world. Together, O'Connor and Percy began a modern Catholic literary tradition in America that continues today.

Since the 1960s that tradition has come into its own. In recent years, American Catholic writers have been among those receiving the highest literary awards in the country. For example, Pulitzer Prizes for Literature went to John Kennedy Toole in 1981 for *A Confederacy of Dunces*, William Kennedy in 1984 for *Ironweed*, and Oscar Hijuelos in 1990 for *The Mambo Kings Play Songs of Love*. In 1997, The National Book Award for general non-fiction went to James Carroll for *An American Requiem*, and the PEN/Faulkner Award for fiction went to Ron Hansen for *Atticus*.

Today, well-known Catholic writers like Hansen and Carroll, Alice McDermott, and Andre Dubus, write about the holiness of everyday life. In their books, readers find themselves on holy ground, even when the stories have to do with the breakup of a marriage or the breakdown of a religious vocation. As writers they are not afraid to voice their doubts, and yet they maintain their belief in a God who loves and forgives and brings meaning to the world. That they are making the right connections is evidenced by their popularity with critics and readers of all faiths.

A Pair of Priests With Pens

Two American Catholic writers whose work regularly appears on bestseller lists are Andrew Greeley and Joseph Girzone. Both are Catholic priests (thought Girzone is no longer in active ministry) and both use their novels to teach lessons of faith. The similarities end there, however.

Greeley, a respected sociologist, writes many popular novels of romance and suspense. By his own admission, Greeley is not trying to write great literature. Instead, he is trying to bring spiritual truths to people who might never consider picking up the Bible or the Catechism (official teaching book) of the Catholic Church.

This is true also of Girzone. His books, particularly his "Joshua" novels, are found in both general and Christian bookstores. Joshua is "Christ come back to Earth" in the person of a simple but wise and miraculous carpenter. The stories tend to be gentle parables that answer the question, "What would Jesus do?" They can be critical of the Catholic establishment and are aimed at a wide Christian readership. Girzone, too, is concerned with spreading the Gospel.

A Cultural Force and the Force of Culture

As Catholics assimilate into the larger culture along with many other groups, distinguishing characteristics fade. Catholics blend in with others. Larger cultural forces influence them, as they do all Americans. The need for a Catholic ghetto is now past. Many attempt to forget that one ever existed.

Blending in speeds up the process of becoming more like everyone else. Fewer and fewer Catholic children attend parish schools. Catholics, outsiders for most of American history, now appear as insiders in so many dimensions that affect the larger American culture. They hold key positions in publishing, the film industry, television and technology, and other industries that influence culture.

The church represents, on the one hand, a cultural force, and on the other, an institution shaped by the force of culture. The church no longer has the impact on culture that it did before Vatican II. But it still is a major presence and influence with its own press, TV, movies, and Internet presence. Meanwhile, MTV, the nightly news, newspapers, books, films, the Internet, advertising, and so many other cultural forces shape the way Catholics think and behave. Society and American culture now have heavy influence on the ways in which Catholicism is viewed by everyone in America.

Catholic Impact
On Social Issues

THE CATHOLIC CHURCH HOLDS STRONG VIEWS ON A NUMBER OF issues that affect society. It defends a strict moral standard. For example, the church teaches that abortion is morally wrong, or sinful. Many American Catholics follow the church's teaching and oppose abortion even though they realize that it is legal under American law. Of course, simply because something may be lawful does not necessarily mean that it is morally right according to Christian principles. Many Catholics want to change the law and make abortion illegal. In this way Catholics are seeking to influence American society.

And yet Catholics are also affected by the larger society in which they live. They adopt the thinking and dispositions of American society. They might find themselves at odds with their own church on a number of issues ranging from the rights of homosexuals to the morality of the death penalty.

The church asks Catholics to follow its teachings whether or not the larger society endorses or agrees with these teachings. However, sometimes Catholics experience conflict between what the church teaches them and what their personal beliefs are. They have to decide whether to follow the church or to rely upon their experience and conscience or act in ways that are contrary to church teaching.

These issues touch the lives of many Americans. They can lead to conflict between the Church and the wider population, and among Catholics themselves. Some of these issues are: capital punishment, economic justice, the conduct of war, marriage and sex, the sacredness of marriage, abortion, bioethics, and health care.

Capital Punishment

Capital punishment, or the death penalty, means that a government puts a convicted criminal to death as punishment for a very serious crime. Many states permit this punishment, but the American Catholic Church opposes it. Official church teaching allows the death penalty in cases of extreme seriousness. Pope John Paul II said that the penalty should be "rare if not practically nonexistent." However, the Catechism (a document of official church teachings) states: "If . . . nonlethal means are enough to defend and protect people's safety, [the state] will limit itself to such means, as these are more in keeping with the common good and [better for] the dignity of the human person."

Many American bishops and cardinals have led a public fight to stop capital punishment. Bishops have gone on record asking for mercy for the accused and urged states to look again at their policies. They argue that the punishment ends all chances of rehabilitation and that only God has the right to take a life.

The bishops fear that America faces a growing trend toward violence—on the streets, in domestic settings, and in our institutions, laws, and public policies. In all cases, the bishops oppose the ability of the state to terminate life.

When the American bishops make statements about public policy, they speak as official representatives of the Catholic Church. It does not necessarily follow that all American Catholics agree with their stance. Indeed, in the case of capital punishment many Catholics disagree with the bishops and favor executions. Supreme Court Justice Antonin Scalia is one prominent Catholic who disagrees with the church's view on capital punishment. Despite these disagreements, the church stands firm against the practice.

Economic Justice

The Catholic Church feels a particular responsibility for the poor. The church addresses this concern in two ways. First, it ministers directly to the poor through soup kitchens, shelters, and health care. The other way that it serves the poor is by being an advocate for them with the government and in the society. The church fights for affordable housing, health care for all Americans, safe schools that provide a decent education, and a living wage for workers.

Throughout its history the Church in America has encouraged the working poor to organize, to bargain collectively, and to seek a fair living wage. The American church's quest for social justice is tied with the Vatican's efforts. Several popes have supported workers. In 1891, Pope Leo XIII wrote a letter supportive of workers' rights and welfare. Fifty years later Pope Pius IX followed up with a similar letter.

In 1986, the American bishops took a bold step when they issued a pastoral letter on the economy. It was called *Economic Justice for All: Catholic Social Teachings and the U. S. Economy*. The letter, written under the leadership of Archbishop Rembert Weakland of Milwaukee, dealt with the moral questions of the American economy. The bishops wrote about a culture that favors the wealthy, spends more on weapons than on welfare, and distributes wealth unevenly. The letter ". . . calls for the establishment of a floor of material well-being on which all can stand" and "calls into question extreme inequalities of income when so many lack basic necessities."

The letter dealt with a wide range of economic issues. These included employment, poverty, food and agriculture, and the role of the United States in a global economy. The bishops argued that individuals have a right to work, and that every effort should be made to provide jobs. They were critical of policies such as overseas manufacturing with lower labor costs, increased spending on high-tech weapons, and lack of job training programs for unskilled workers. The bishops deplored the fact that one in seven Americans, including many children, lives in poverty amid so much wealth. They also called for improvements to the welfare system.

As bold as this American letter was, it was following the universal church. In 1981, Pope John Paul II defended work for every individual as a God-given right, along with the right of workers to form legitimate unions. So the American bishops built on an established tradition.

They had spoken on similar topics in the past (on unemployment in 1930, on the social order in 1940, and the economy as recently as 1970). However, this was the first time that the bishops addressed American

WHY NOT?

In a December 2001 statement, the American bishops noted that the United States is the only Western industrialized nation today that uses capital punishment as a form of justice. They said:

There are compelling reasons for opposing capital punishment—its sheer inhumanity and its absolute finality, as well as concern about its [unequal] use and an imperfect legal system that has sentenced innocent people to death. Executing the guilty does not honor one who was killed, nor does it [lift up] the living or even lessen their pain, for only love and forgiveness can do that. State-sanctioned killing affects us all because it diminishes the value we place on all human life. Capital punishment also cuts short the guilty person's opportunity for spiritual conversion and repentance.

society as a whole on this topic. This showed that American Catholics and their leaders no longer thought it necessary to support American public policy no matter what. The Catholic community in America was no longer an immigrant one seeking to prove its patriotism. It had risen above suspicion that it was loyal to a foreign power in Rome. These letters on the economy symbolically represent an American Catholic community coming of age.

Weapons and War

From the Civil War to the War on Terrorism, Americans have fought one another and our common enemies in war. The church has had a well-developed theory of "just war" (war fought for a good reason) since the 12th century. The theory says that people or nations are permitted to defend themselves by the use of force if an opponent intends to do them serious harm or kill them. The use of force must be appropriate for each case, however. One should not use more force than is necessary for each situation.

With the development of nuclear weapons, many people began to believe that any use of such weapons went beyond appropriate force. These weapons are so powerful that the damage they do cannot be confined to soldiers in war but can wipe out entire cities. Many innocent people are likely to be killed in a nuclear attack.

In 1983 the American bishops addressed the issue of war in a letter titled *The Challenge of Peace*. They urged America to slow down the arms race and not to resort to war as a means to resolve conflicts. The letter was addressed to all Americans, not just Catholics. The bishops consulted many different groups for their input. These included scientists, the military, government officials, scholars, and ordinary Americans, both Catholic and non-Catholic. One of the committee members, Cardinal John O'Connor of New York, held the rank of admiral in the U.S. Navy and had served as the bishop for U. S. armed forces.

Some Catholics disagreed strongly with the document's position that first-strike nuclear war (that is, being the first in a conflict to use a nuclear weapon) cannot be justified under any conditions. In general, conservatives inside and outside the church disagreed with the bishops. More liberal people agreed with the document. Those within the church were encouraged by the support for the document in circles outside the church.

Marriage and Divorce

The sacrament of marriage is one that Catholic couples look forward to with great hope and anticipation. Marriage is also a time when they want all of the pageantry and ceremony that a sacramental celebration affords. Curiously, even those who have not been to church for years want to be married in a church. This may simply be because of the setting—a church is more solemn and traditional than the court chambers of a judge. Or it may have more to do with the wishes of the parents than those of the couple to be married. To please parents and relatives, couples want to come before the altar. Or it may be something deeper, something sacred, something holy that inspires them to seek the sacrament of matrimony. They want their vows to one another to be sacred, to be blessed by God, to be witnessed publicly by the Catholic and Christian community.

As with the other sacraments, the parish is the connection with the larger Church. Through the parish couples are prepared for marriage. Marriage is the only sacrament that is not actually given by a priest or deacon. Instead, a priest or deacon "witnesses" the marriage, while the bride and groom actually complete the sacrament together.

Many contemporary Catholic couples are more influenced by American culture than by church doctrine when it comes to marriage. The age of first marriages has been steadily rising since the 1990s. Young people are not likely to make a commitment to marriage until they have finished their education and settled into a career pattern.

The idea of living together before marriage was frowned upon for many years, but today is quite normal. Officially the church disapproves of such practices and considers people in such arrangements to be sinners. In practice, however, many Catholics get married in the Church despite their living arrangements. The couple may not be coming to church or living in a wholesome union in the eyes of the church, but turning them away from the altar at the time of marriage may alienate them for the rest of their married lives. Many priests are reluctant to risk creating such bad feelings. However, some priests, having judged that this has already occurred, do end up turning away the couple.

The sad underside of marriage is divorce. Catholics divorce at the same rate as other Americans. However, the church does not recognize divorce. Referring to the marriage bond, Jesus said: "What God has joined together let no one separate." For Catholics marriage is not only a contract, it is a sacrament. And sacraments cannot be canceled. The church, however, can annul marriages. These "annulments" mean that a sacrament was never conferred, that the marriage never happened in the eyes of the church. The legal, non-Catholic part of a marriage can be ended by a civil divorce issued in the courts. The annulment process, however, does not affect the civil status of the marriage, and the children from an annulled marriage are legitimate.

There are many reasons for the church to grant an annulment, including the immaturity of one or both of the parties at the time of marriage. The most common reason that the church annuls marriages is "psychological incapacity." This is related not to age but to the maturity, understanding, and ability of a person to enter into a permanent bond. If at the time of marriage a person was not mature enough to understand and accept the sacramental bond of marriage, after proper investigation and procedures, the church can annul that marriage. Thousands of marriages are annulled each year in church tribunals. More annulments are granted in America than anywhere else.

All types of misconceptions surround the annulment process, from the idea that only rich or famous people obtain them to the perception that the church is getting rich in the annulment "business." The fact is that anyone who was married in the church may apply for an annulment and the vast majority of annulments are granted to ordinary Catholics who pay a nominal fee to defray some of the costs of processing their request.

Pre-Marital Sex

The importance of marriage, as reflected above, leads to another important Catholic social teaching regarding sexual relations. The church understands that young people experience strong temptations to be sexually active, and that some are sexually active. However, the church opposes sexual intercourse for anyone outside of marriage. Some of the thinking behind this belief is echoed in these lines from the pamphlet *Love Waits*, which was developed by the Southern Baptist Convention but approved also by the Catholic Church:

> Love is patient, love is kind. Love wants what is best for another person. Love never demands something that will harm you or the person you love. Love will never cross the line between what's right and wrong. It's wrong to put one another in danger of having to deal with hard choices—choices that could change your lives, your goals, and your plans forever. Having sex before marriage may feel right for the moment. But the possible costs of an unexpected pregnancy, abortion, and sexually transmitted disease— as well as the deep hurts that can come from a broken relationship—outweigh the feelings of the moment. The feelings are temporary; their consequences are long-lasting.

All good things are worth waiting for, the church teaches. Waiting until marriage to have sexual relations is a mature decision to control one's desires. The church asks its members to abstain from sexual intercourse before marriage. Abstinence (which means not taking part) from sex allows young people to develop physically and to mature emotionally and spiritually in preparation for marriage. The Catholic Church says: If it's love, love waits. For many young Catholics, this is one of the hardest issues they face in making their faith part of their lives.

Birth Control

Along these same lines, the church has teachings about the use of birth-control devices or medicines to prevent pregnancy. In 1967, Pope Paul VI established a commission to study whether or not the church should permit Catholics to use birth control. On July 29, 1968, against the recommendation of the commission, which wanted to permit it, Pope Paul VI confirmed in a special letter the Church's rules against any form of artificial birth control for Catholics. This struck a sensitive chord in Catholic couples' lives. While the church continued to permit—even encourage—what it called "natural family planning," the use of artificial means to prohibit conception, including birth control pills, was deemed sinful.

Historically, many papal letters are little known or noticed by Catholics. This one created a firestorm. This letter forced many American Catholics to choose between what their church was teaching and what their conscience told them. The emotional and financial expense of having large families was more than many could bear. They were not denying the value of human life, but they were reluctant to bring children into the world for whom they could not adequately provide and care. American Catholics largely ignored the teaching and practiced birth control.

Praying for social change
Often, Catholic youth groups come together to protest or pray together for a change in a social policy they see as wrong. In this 1999 photo, a group prays on the steps of the U.S. Supreme Court to promote the group's anti-abortion message.

AIDS Prevention

The church is concerned about AIDS yet, since it opposes all forms of birth control, it does not approve of the use of condoms to prevent the spread of AIDS. Instead, it recommends abstinence to its followers. However, the church is painfully aware of the devastating consequences of AIDS. Among efforts to comfort the afflicted and to inform its people a U.S. bishops' group produced a video titled *Living with AIDS: An Occasion of Grace* which they describe on their Web site as follows:

> The devastation of AIDS has affected countless lives in the United States. In health care facilities and outreach programs across the nation, Catholics are offering their hands and hearts to persons living with AIDS. From a home for HIV-positive mothers in Los Angeles to a support group in New York, *Living with AIDS introduces us to some of these people: a teen group that uses dramatizations to educate peers about AIDS prevention; parishioners who do household chores for neighbors living with AIDS; a hemophiliac, who lost his wife and most of his family to AIDS; and members of a South Dakota parish dealing with the denial and discrimination surrounding the death of a friend by AIDS. The video demonstrates how individuals can make a difference in healing the physical, emotional, and spiritual scars brought on by the AIDS epidemic.*

The church's rules about sex are clearly contrary to the thinking of most of society. But this does not imply that the church should change its thinking. It means that it faces a more difficult task proclaiming and enforcing its sexual moral code. Many Catholics do not take the code seriously; or, if they disagree with it, they have developed ways to feel okay about what they do. In the view of some Catholics, the church's position renders it out of date in a world that tolerates all manner of sexual relationships. Yet the church consistently opposes lifestyles for Catholics that undermine the sacramental nature of marriage and sexual morality.

The Church and Homosexuals

In recent decades in America, homosexuality has become a controversial issue affecting many parts of our culture. The gay rights movement has been very active since the 1960s, lobbying governments for legal recognition of gay couples and for more rights for gay people. They have asked for equal treatment within society, business, and even churches. The Catholic Church, however, believes that all sexual unions should have the chance to produce children. Thus, human beings, they believe, should only have sexual relationships with the opposite gender. This position has led to conflict.

In some cases, it has also led to violence. The church speaks out strongly against such violence against homosexuals. However, it has actively campaigned against equal rights for gays. In 1992, American bishops wrote a pastoral letter that stressed the potential harm to society if certain non-discrimination laws are passed. The bishops urged Catholic voters to take this into consideration when making their choices about political candidates. In a 1994 letter the bishops encouraged homosexuals not to be sexually active. In 1997 they published a letter, *Always Our Children*, that reminded parents of homosexuals to continue to love their children, and church ministers to treat homosexuals compassionately.

Part of the church's concern involves marriage. If gay couples receive the same benefits as those of married people, the church views this as endorsing homosexual relationships and putting them on the level of marriage. The church believes that marriage should be reserved only for unions between a man and a woman. Gay sexual relationships cannot produce offspring, and the church believes that sexual relationships should be open to the possibility of children. The church recognizes that some married couples cannot have children, but not necessarily by choice. It considers homosexual activity sinful and does not wish to see the government, businesses, or social groups approve of it.

As with other issues on which the church takes a firm stance, not all Catholics agree with church officials. American Catholics are as divided about the homosexual lifestyle as almost any other large national group. Certainly there are Catholics active in the gay community. Many of these are conflicted about their relationship to the church.

Abortion

Abortion is perhaps the most controversial issue with which the Church deals. Many Americans view abortion as a purely private matter for a woman to decide. The United States Supreme Court protected women's rights to abortion in the Roe vs. Wade ruling in 1973 (see the box, opposite). Both sides of the issue consider abortion as a moral matter of making the right choice.

Perhaps the key issue is just who should have the power to decide whether abortion is allowed. Pro-life people (those against abortion) feel that the state should not have a role in that decision, either for or against. Pro-choice people (those for the ability of women to decide whether or not to have an abortion) feel that the state should not put up barriers to that decision. The Catholic Church considers abortion a grave sin that can separate a Catholic permanently from the church.

Ever since the 1973 ruling, the Catholic Church has been fighting to overturn it and make abortion illegal in America. The church believes the fetus (unborn child) to be a human being from the moment of conception. Thus, it holds that no one can end that life, no matter what the reason. It actively supports the anti-abortion movement and attempts to influence the courts and the government to stop abortion. In these efforts, the Catholic Church often joins evangelical Christian churches and conservative groups.

American bishops speak out against abortion. They even hired a public relations company to help them get their message out. Catholic college professors banded together to bring the message to campuses. The church works with political parties and politicians, too. On the local level, parishes and priests work with community groups and with pregnant women, all in an effort to end abortion. Each January, thousands of Catholics and others take part in the March for Life in Washington, D.C. They hear speeches and join in protests against abortion and the laws that make it legal.

Not all Catholics follow the church's teaching, however, and neither do some Catholic politicians. Prominent figures such as Geraldine Ferraro, who ran for vice president in 1984, former Governor Mario Cuomo of New York, and Senator Edward Kennedy of Massachusetts all believe that they must support the law of the land even if this contradicts church teaching.

The church continues to oppose all forms of abortion. It teaches its members that regardless of the law, Catholics should not undergo or support abortions in any way. To support pregnant women, the church funds counseling centers, offers alternatives such as adoption, and provides prenatal health care. The battle over abortion rights is perhaps one of the most important focuses of American Catholic efforts in the social and political arenas.

Bioethics

Bioethics looks at the ethics of medical procedures. For example, should we clone animals and humans? Should we genetically engineer organs for transplant? Should we be able to choose the traits of babies?

WHAT IS ROE VS. WADE?

That is the name of the 1973 U.S. Supreme Court decision that ruled that abortion was legal in the United States. That decision has been hotly debated ever since. On one side are "pro-life" supporters, who are against abortion and who seek to limit abortions or make them illegal. On the other are "pro-choice" supporters, who feel it is the woman's right to choose and that right should not be restricted.

Two separate issues are involved in bioethics. The first involves the ability to create human beings. The second issue is whether or not we should make changes to humans on a genetic scale. This is not a scientific issue but an ethical concern. Some think that scientists have no right to "play God" by deciding such critical matters as who lives and who dies. Both Presidents Bill Clinton and George W. Bush have opposed unrestricted manipulation of humans by science and medicine. The church joins them in warning scientists that the ability to do something does not necessarily mean that it is right to do so.

The American bishops' pro-life activities committee acts as a watchdog over the medical community and the legislature. In 2001 the bishops supported legislation against human cloning. The bishops also oppose stem-cell research (using cells from fetuses) on the grounds that the tissues used in these procedures can sometimes come from abortions. They say research cannot destroy life in order to enhance life.

The church also opposes physician-assisted suicide. Some people argue that terminally ill people should have the right to end their lives with the help of a doctor. The church believes that only God may have that power, even for what some may view as reasons of compassion. No patient, no family, and no doctor should decide who lives or dies or assist someone to end his or her own life, says the church. This does not mean that the church does not approve of the use of pain-killing medications. However, assisting in a death constitutes a moral offense.

Health Care

Every day Catholic hospitals and nursing homes serve millions of patients in America. The Catholic Church operates more than 1,000 hospitals and health-care centers serving 80 million patients annually. The church participates in the health care system because in the Gospel, Jesus says his followers are supposed to take care of the sick. Following in Jesus' footsteps, the church has developed an elaborate system of hospitals, nursing homes, hospices (a place for dying people), and other health care facilities.

In the 19th century, religious sisters offered a high degree of personal care for patients in hospitals, including those with incurable diseases. The story is told of a visitor to a leper hospital who saw a nun changing the bandages of a patient. "I wouldn't do that for a million

dollars!" he said in disgust. "Sir," answered the sister, "neither would I."
Today, with technology dominating health care, nuns and other Catholic
health care providers focus on the spiritual part of healing, too.

As early as 1727, sisters came to America to minister to the sick
when 12 French Ursuline nuns arrived in New Orleans. By the 1960s,
there were about 860 Catholic hospitals in the United States. Along with
serving patients with traditional insurance and government payments,
the church provides medical care free of charge for those without insurance. By 1975 the number of Catholic hospitals declined to 671, and

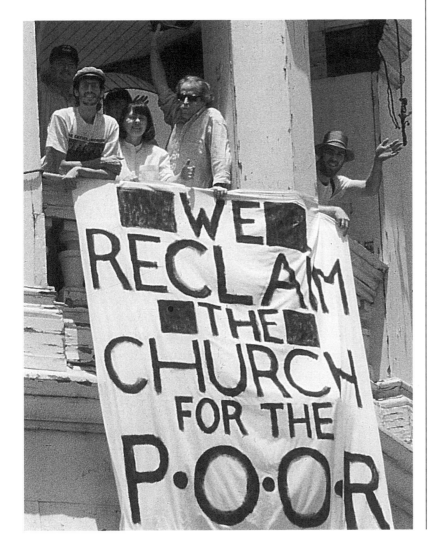

Offering a helping hand
Protests such as this one in
1995 by the Catholic Worker
in Los Angeles are just one
of the ways that Catholic
people and groups work
together to help those in
society, either directly or by
raising awareness or
consciousness of the
problems.

the number of nuns working in them dropped from 13,618 to 8,980. Today, Catholic health care facilities employ about 700,000 Americans. In Catholic hospitals spiritual care is now provided by teams of priests, nuns, and laypeople. The hospital staff and patients are changing, too, becoming more and more non-Catholic.

Catholic Charities

The church takes its obligation to care for the poor seriously. As a result of this commitment, it has built a system of social services for the needy. Often local parishes provide these services. Most churches have what is called a "poor box" into which Catholics contribute money. These funds provide for various needs within and beyond the parish. When Catholics face economic hardship, they can turn to their local parish for help. Pastors can provide emergency aid to individuals and families. Usually they carry out this ministry quietly and without fanfare, but it means a lifeline for those who need help right away.

Beyond this personal assistance, parishes provide organizing help through social action committees. These parish programs support everything from soup kitchens to refugee relocation. Most operate year-

Operation Rice Bowl

American Catholics help not only in their own country, but overseas as well. Through Catholic Relief Services (CRS), the American Church supports projects all over the globe. Developing nations often need money and help to advance their society. CRS provides funds, experts, and ideas to countries in need, whether because of war, drought, poverty, or other troubles.

Catholic school children help to fund CRS by contributing money through a program called Operation Rice Bowl. During the holy season of Lent, the 40 days preparing for Easter, Catholics are asked to make sacrifices. School children receive "Rice Bowls," small cardboard boxes in which they can put aside some of their allowance and earnings to aid the poor of the world. The church holds a special collection each year to gather the money saved in these rice bowls and combine it with a national collection sponsored by the bishops.

Through CRS the American church makes it plain that American Catholics have a responsibility to care for those less fortunate, no matter where in the world they are found. The church does not specifically target Catholics to help, but offers assistance to those who truly need it, no matter their nationality, race, or religion.

round, though they may be most visible during the Christmas season when many distribute food baskets for families and toys for needy children. Often they work in the general community, too.

Each diocese also has social service agencies. Usually called Catholic Charities, these agencies serve various social needs, including health care, legal aid, counseling, foster care, adoption services, food, and shelter, among others. Nationally, the Roman Catholic Church distributes hundreds of millions of dollars each year to its organizations that care for those in need.

Of course, Catholics are not alone in their efforts to assist the poor, the troubled, and the needy. Other Christian churches do the same, as well as Jewish relief agencies, and Islamic, Hindu, and Buddhist communities. While some object to church-state cooperation, faith-based agencies can offer a natural vehicle for the government to reach those most in need.

The impact that the church has on American society, with its extensive system of aid, cannot be fully estimated. The church cares for the material as well as the spiritual needs of millions of Americans each year, many of whom are not Catholic. For example, in caring for the poor and the homeless, the church does not discriminate between Catholics and others, or even between believers and non-believers. All are welcome. By and large, these programs do not attempt to convert participants to Catholicism. Instead, they demonstrate the care and compassion that Jesus asked his followers to have, regardless of the beliefs or lack of beliefs of those they serve. A hungry person is a hungry person, whether he or she is Catholic or not. The church's mission is to feed the hungry, to clothe the naked, to comfort the afflicted, not to question their religious affiliation or lack thereof.

5

Catholics and American Politics

THE PARTICIPATION OF CATHOLICS IN THE POLITICAL PROCESS HAS varied during American history. For a long time Catholics had little political influence because of the discrimination they suffered. Some observers think that the first serious Catholic candidate for the presidency, Al Smith, the governor of New York, lost the 1928 election to Herbert Hoover because Smith was a Catholic. Many citizens were reluctant to vote for Smith because they feared that the pope would exercise authority over him and he therefore would not be free to make decisions on his own.

With so many members and institutions within American society—such as schools, hospitals, homeless shelters, day care centers, nursing homes, and social services for the needy—the Catholic Church is a powerful social force. Elected officials often consider the church's position on issues when forming policies. Some Catholics actively lobby elected officials to express their views, led by Catholic teaching, on a number of public policies. The church does not always prevail in these efforts, but it offers its views on issues that have moral implications. For example, the church opposes capital punishment on moral grounds (see page 70), but many states continue to execute death row inmates despite protests by ordinary Catholics and officials of the Catholic Church.

Catholics in Public Life

The fear that a person's Catholic faith might interfere with his or her work in government has come up time and again in American history. Here are some prominent examples.

John F. Kennedy, the first and only Catholic president, won a very close election in 1961. During the campaign he was forced to defend his patriotism and his Catholicism. The media questioned whether he would govern according to the Catholic Church's view or whether he could act independently of his faith. In a speech to the Texas Baptist Ministerial Association, Kennedy forcefully asserted that his religion would not interfere with his duties as president. He calmed the fears of those who thought he would consult the pope on political matters.

Supreme Court Justice William J. Brennan Jr. faced a similar trial some years earlier. In 1956, the Senate committee investigating his nomination to the court asked if he could be both a good Catholic and good American. Brennan assured the committee that in his court decisions he would be governed exclusively by his oath to uphold the Constitution. In a number of instances during his stay on the Court, Brennan confirmed this by voting for laws that the church did not favor.

Former New York Republican mayor Rudolph Giuliani, *Time* magazine's Person of the Year in 2001, is a lifelong Catholic. He served as mayor of the country's largest city in a state that is 44 percent Catholic. In 1999 Giuliani strongly protested an art display called *Sensations* planned for the Brooklyn Museum because he objected to the exhibit on moral grounds. The museum, which receives public funds, wanted to exhibit a painting by a little-known British artist depicting Mary, the mother of Jesus. The composition of the painting included cow dung on the body of Mary. Catholics were outraged and Giuliani shared their anger, referring to the exhibit as "sick stuff." Demanding cancellation of the show, Giuliani said, "You don't have a right to government [money] for desecrating [or ridiculing] somebody else's religion, and therefore we will do everything that we can to remove funding."

Giuliani faced criticism for mixing his beliefs into politics. The press mostly came out against him. New York residents disagreed with his actions by a margin of two to one in a poll. Eventually, the courts sided with the museum and allowed the exhibit. But it was an example of a politician walking the thin line between faith and civic duty.

RUDY RUDY RUDY

Speaking his mind
Before his vital role in helping the nation heal after
September 11, 2001, New
York mayor Rudoph Giuliani
was involved in several issues in which his Catholic
beliefs clashed with his role
as a civic leader.

Though he was against using public funds in the museum case, in another case that involved religion, Giuliani supported using public funds. The money would be used for school vouchers, which would go to parents to use as they saw fit, sending their children to any school they chose. Many of those vouchers, or payments, would go to religious schools. In this case, the public did not speak against him for mixing personal faith and politics.

In 1984, President Ronald Reagan and Pope John Paul II agreed to have the United States represented in the Vatican by an ambassador. Since then, Catholics have filled the position. One of them, Raymond Flynn, drew unwanted attention to the job. In 1994, Flynn, a former mayor of Boston, was appointed by President Clinton as U.S. ambassador to the Vatican. From the Vatican, Flynn denounced Congressional Republicans in a letter to U. S. religious leaders for what he claimed were violations of Catholic social teaching. In the 1996 letter, Flynn criticized the Republican majority in Congress. He claimed that their plans for budget cuts went against Pope John Paul II's teachings, including statements the pope made during his 1995 visit to the United States.

The U. S. Inspector General, a Congressional watchdog agency, objected to his comments. The Secretary of State, Warren Christopher, publicly chastised Flynn for expressing his personal views in a way that made his comments look like U.S. government policy. Christopher warned Flynn not to inject his personal religious views into political debates. Flynn shocked the government again when he announced that he disagreed with the president's decision to allow a certain type of abortion. In 1997, Flynn was replaced by Rep. Lindy Boggs.

Catholics and Political Parties

For generations Catholics favored the policies of the Democratic Party. The politics of the Democrats supported ordinary working persons and plenty of Catholics fit that description. The Democratic Party identified with the concerns of immigrants and outsiders. It had found a strong base of support among Catholics since the middle of the 19th century. For example, Catholics overwhelmingly supported President Franklin D. Roosevelt's New Deal policies in the 1930s. These gave jobs to blue-collar workers. As working class people, Catholics looked to the Democratic Party to represent their interests. Trade unions supported Democratic candidates locally and nationally. Even today most large labor unions support the Democratic candidate for president.

For decades, Democratic politicians could count on the support and the votes of working-class Catholics. In certain locations around the country with large concentrations of Catholics, the Democrats fared well in both local and national elections. The Northeast, with a large Catholic population, has been a stronghold of the Democratic Party. Other traditionally industrial cities, such as Detroit and St. Louis, regularly voted for majority Democrats. Since 1931, all of the mayors of the city of Chicago have been Democrats.

Throughout much of the 20th century "the Catholic vote" usually favored Democratic candidates. In the past three decades, however, this has changed. As Catholics have become better educated and wealthier, they have increasingly split their vote between Democrats and Republicans. Recent Catholic immigrants maintain the working-class character of Catholicism, but many of them do not vote. This can be either because they are illegally in the United States, or because their immigration status does not allow them to vote, or because they simply choose not to.

Another factor is the position of the Democratic Party on social and moral issues. Many Democratic candidates favor liberal abortion

CATHOLICS IN GOVERNMENT

Here are some of the most prominent Catholics in American government today:

Supreme Court Justices **Antonin Scalia** (see page 104), **Clarence Thomas,** and **Anthony Kennedy**

Sen. Edward Kennedy (D-Massachusetts)

Sen. Tom Harkin (D-Iowa)

Sen. John Kerry (D-Massachusetts)

Sen. Tom Daschle (D-North Dakota)

Sen. Patty Murray (D-Washington)

Gov. George Pataki (R-New York)

Gov. Gray Davis (D-California)

Tom Ridge (director of homeland security)

Rep. Nancy Pelosi (D-California)

laws. Catholics who strongly oppose abortion are unlikely to vote for them. For a variety of reasons, Catholic voters are more unpredictable today than in the past and can no longer be counted on to favor one political party on a regular basis.

Lobbying Efforts

The Catholic Church, like other social and political groups, tries to influence public policy to favor its positions. The church actively lobbies, or tries to convince, the government to favor policies that respect human life, care for the poor, bring justice to society, and permit religious freedom. The church acts on the local, national, and international level. The United States Conference of Catholic Bishops (USCCB) organizes these activities. The USCCB encourages those policies and laws that will promote Catholic values. They write, "Our moral framework does not easily fit the categories of right or left, Democrat or Republican. Our responsibility is to measure every party and platform by how its agenda touches human life and dignity."

However, they do express opinions about several political issues that affect the American people. They speak out about the life and dignity of the person, the family, the rights of workers, the environment, social justice, and war. They offer direction on international policies as well. They address issues such as debt relief for developing nations, immigration policies, and human rights. In the area of immigration, for example, the bishops advocate a policy that will permit a temporary or permanent safe haven for those in need. They seek to protect immigrant workers, help families stay together, and allow families to return to their homeland.

The bishops also maintain a government liaison office, representing the Catholic Church before Congress. Every two years it prepares a list of issues it would like to have Congress talk about. For example, it looks at proposals to introduce values education into public schools. It also has an office for social development and world peace. The office creates programs and produces literature for use in parishes. It suggests ways that Catholics can oppose what the church calls a "culture of violence," by fighting racism, stopping domestic violence, opposing the death penalty, and promoting the church's pro-life ideas.

The migration and refugee services arm of the USCCB provides services and advice to immigrants and refugees. They work with the

CATHOLIC VOTE IN PRESIDENTIAL ELECTIONS

This chart shows the Democrat/Republican split of the Catholic vote in elections since 1948.

Year	Catholic Vote Dem/Rep
1948	65/ 35
1952	51/49
1956	45/55
1960	82/18
1964	78/22
1968	55/37
1972	37/63
1976	56/44
1980	40/51
1984	44/56
1988	52/48
1992*	48/29
1996	55/38
2000	50/47

*In 1992, 22 percent of Catholic voters voted for a third-party candidate.

Leader of U.S. bishops
In 2001, Bishop Wilton Gregory, from a diocese near St. Louis, became the president of the USCCB. He is the first African-American to hold this important post.

federal government and local communities to settle refugees and provide basic services for immigrants.

In 2001, another USCCB committee wrote an important paper that drew attention to the promise and the problems of Africa. The document noted the many signs of hope in Africa and pointed out that Christianity is growing rapidly there. But Africa remains plagued by poverty, civil war, AIDS, political oppression, and conflict between religions. The church is encouraging Americans to care for and assist their brothers and sisters in areas such as Africa, where they desperately need resources.

The USCCB also has an office that provides help to the countries of the former Soviet Union. This help goes directly towards rebuilding the church in these former Communist lands, but even this effort has political overtones. Many of these countries struggle to survive as independent nations and the church aids their efforts while encouraging them to return to their Christian roots.

Because the American church is well off financially, American Catholics feel an obligation to contribute to the church elsewhere and to support human rights and development everywhere. American Catholics have been very generous to church appeals for help with international crises, recognizing their own good fortune and feeling compelled by the Gospel to share their blessings with those less fortunate at home and abroad.

The Catholic League

In 1973 Father Virgil C. Blum, S.J., founded the Catholic League for Religious and Civil Rights. The group defends the right of Catholics to participate in American public life without defamation or discrimination. Motivated by the First Amendment, the Catholic League attempts to protect religious freedom and the free speech of Catholics. Whenever someone speaks out unfairly against the Catholic Church, the Catholic League responds through the public media to defend the Church. Aware of the history of anti-Catholicism in America, this group acts as a watchdog against wrongful representations of the Church in public culture. It also defends the right of the Church to promote its teachings.

In the 1990s, it was was very active, encouraging Catholics to boycott some events or organizations. In 1997, it asked Catholics not to watch the television show *Nothing Sacred*, which featured what the league saw as an uncomplimentary plot about a Catholic parish. In 2001, it wrote to a major food company asking it not to sponsor a radio show the league found offensive. The league has not been afraid to go to court to correct what it views as unfair views of the church in the media or unfair treatment of Catholics in public life or the workplace.

The Catholic League compares itself to the NAACP (National Association for the Advancement of Colored People), established to protect the rights of African-Americans, and the ADL (Anti-Defamation League), designed to protect Jews. The league often find itself in the media because it tackles difficult and highly visible cases.

One School's Plan

Many of the efforts that Catholics make to improve society are local initiatives. Most parishes have social action or peace and justice committees that coordinate activities of the parishioners. Catholic schools

MAKING A DIFFERENCE
The Catholic Campaign for Human Development, supported by an annual collection in churches, funds projects in states, cities, and neighborhoods to serve the poor and to encourage self-development. The effort has funded more than 4,000 programs across the United States, fighting poverty locally and bringing social justice to those without a voice in the political process.

The campaign has two objectives: The first is to raise money to support "organized groups of white and minority poor to develop economic strength and political power." The second is to "educate the People of God to a new knowledge of today's problems . . . that can lead to some new approaches that promote a greater sense of solidarity."

also train their students to be good citizens by integrating community action projects into the school week. For example, at Stone Ridge School of the Sacred Heart, an all-girls Catholic school in Bethesda, Maryland, students participate in social action projects each week as part of their curriculum. Formal academic classes end at noon each Wednesday to permit students to participate in outreach projects that help local communities.

The program serves two purposes: It offers help to the community, and students learn the habit of volunteering their time and skills. The ninth grade students remain on campus to do a variety of activities, such as making sandwiches for a homeless shelter. Other weeks they have a speaker or view a movie or have a discussion about Catholics in society and politics.

Those in the upper high school visit hospitals and nursing homes, tutor elementary school children, serve food at a soup kitchen, assist the mentally or physically challenged, or work with the poor. Every student also learns cardio-pulmonary resuscitation (CPR). Teachers as well as students participate in the program.

These activities may not appear obviously political. The idea, however, is to create a more compassionate society and to teach students responsibility to their community to put gospel values into action for others. Students are taught that creating a just society requires personal involvement, not simply voting.

Grassroots Efforts

Pax Christi (Latin for "peace of Christ"), a Catholic peace movement, began in 1972 in the United States. The movement started in France in 1945 to pray for peace. Now part of an international movement, a U.S. office in Pennsylvania serves 14,000 members. The members pray and work for peace. They hope to transform society through nonviolence. They produce a number of publications that both inform their members and instruct followers on how to conduct civil disobedience.

Individuals commit to nonviolence in their personal and family lives and work to influence society to do the same. Part of this political work revolves around their efforts to convince the United States government to abandon its build-up of weapons. The organization calls on the military to disarm. It urges that international disputes be resolved not by war but by dialogue through organizations such as the

United Nations. Pax Christi also advocates economic justice and interracial equality.

Members of this organization sometimes confront authorities in peaceful protests that lead to their arrest. Considered radical by some observers, they gladly accept this description since they believe that the Gospel demands radical action and does not invite us to a comfortable life of inaction. The action they undertake is rooted in prayer and reflection and grounded in the Gospel.

Conclusion

Like every other religious group in America, Catholics participate in the political process. The institutional church regularly takes positions on issues that have moral implications. Not all Catholics follow the church's lead, often taking their own course. Nevertheless, the church consistently urges that Americans—both Catholics and others—consider its values and principles. The church participates in the political process both by suggesting a direction for the country and by actively engaging in issues.

Important American Catholics

CATHOLIC LEADERS HAVE HELPED TO SHAPE THE AMERICAN landscape in the past and many are influential today. Their Catholic faith inspired them, and they in turn inspired and influenced American society. Catholic and non-Catholics in America probably know many of the people described in this chapter. These people contributed, or continue to contribute, to the nation as well as the church. They represent some of the most celebrated figures in American Catholicism.

John Carroll (1735–1815)

John Carroll was bishop of Baltimore, the first bishop in the founding diocese of the church in the United States. He was born in Maryland in 1735. Carroll's father was born in Ireland and his mother, from a wealthy family, was educated in France. At the age of 12, Carroll studied at a Jesuit school in Cecil County, Maryland, for one year, after which he studied for six years in France. At the age of 34, he was ordained a priest and began teaching in France and England. Then, in 1773, Pope Clement XIV suppressed the Jesuits, putting Carroll out of a job.

In 1774 he returned to Maryland where, because of laws discriminating against Catholics, there was no public Catholic Church. He built a small chapel on his mother's land where he said Mass and continued his scholarly life. In 1776, he accompanied some members of the Continental Congress to Canada to try to secure the neutrality of Canada, which was mainly Catholic, during the War of Independence. After the Revolutionary War, Carroll and five other priests met at Whitemarsh, Maryland, on June 6, 1783, to discuss the future of the Catholic Church. A year later, they met and drafted rules for priests in Maryland.

On June 6, 1784, the pope confirmed Carroll's selection as Superior of the Missions in the 13 United States of North America. At the time of his appointment, the Catholic Church in Maryland was composed of 9,000 freemen, 3,000 children, and 3,000 slaves, served by 19 priests. Carroll settled in Baltimore and became the first bishop in America on November 6, 1789, when Pope Pius VI appointed him.

Carroll established schools to train priests, including St. Mary's College and Seminary, and Georgetown College to educate people of all faiths. He ordained the first priests from the original 13 colonies and guided the American Church through its early years in difficult times for Catholics, until his death in Baltimore on December 3, 1815.

John Hughes (1797–1864)

Born in Ireland on June 24, 1797, John J. Hughes came to the United Sates in 1817. Ordained in 1826, he moved to Pennsylvania to work. In 1833 he founded the *Catholic Herald* newspaper and was appointed a bishop in New York in 1838. There he fought a losing battle for the rights of Catholic children to enter the city's public school system. That defeat led him to found an independent Catholic school system that would become one of the best in the country. He also wrestled power away from the laity, or parish members. He put church property under the control of the bishop, not the lay trustees, who were members of the parish.

In the 1840s, Hughes vigorously opposed the Know-Nothing political party, which opposed Catholics immigrating to America. After anti-Catholic riots in Philadelphia in 1844, he prevailed upon the mayor of New York to prohibit rallies that he knew would result in civil unrest. He told New York Mayor Robert Morris "if a single Catholic church is burned in New York, the city will become Moscow," referring to the fires that the Russians had set in 1812 to stop the advances of the invading French army then led by Napoleon Bonaparte.

Ironically, Hughes later represented the United States in France in 1861 to explain the American Civil War to Napoleon. He successfully secured Napoleon's support for the Union and not the Confederacy. When there were more riots in New York in 1863, he addressed the rioters and helped to end the turmoil.

The New York archdiocese grew under his leadership. He had the foresight to build St. Patrick's Cathedral (see page 41) in a part of New York that was considered "in the country" at the time but is now the heart of the city. At the time, critics labeled the cathedral "Hughes' folly," but it became an enduring symbol of the place American Catholics held in the nation. Bishop Hughes was a powerful and influential figure in the American church hierarchy, a role his successors in New York enjoy to this day.

Katharine Drexel (1858–1955)

Only the second American-born person to be named a saint, Katharine Drexel lived a rich life as a wealthy heiress and later as a nun. Drexel was born in 1858 into a wealthy Philadelphia family. Her mother, Hannah, passed away one month after her birth, and her father, Francis, a well-known banker and philanthropist, later married Emma Bouvier. In 1870, Francis Drexel purchased a summer home, Saint Michel, in Torresdale, Pennsylvania. There Katharine and her sister, Elizabeth, taught at a Sunday school that Emma Drexel began for the children of employees and neighbors. They often helped their mother serve the poor.

In her 20s, when she was caring for her mother who was dying of cancer, Drexel felt called to religious life. After her father's death in 1885, Drexel inherited a great sum of money. She wanted to serve the poor directly so she used her fortune to minister to the less fortunate.

At about the same time she became aware of the plight of Native Americans on reservations and problems in the black communities around Philadelphia. She provided moral and financial support to the Bureau of Colored and Indian Missions that helped the poor nationally and internationally. She built 14 boarding schools on reservations, in the rural South, and in urban areas in nine different states. She gave more than money, however. She visited the poor where they lived on the reservations, brought them much needed supplies, and built schools for them in which she paid the teachers. In 1889, she joined an order of religious women, the Sisters of the Blessed Sacrament.

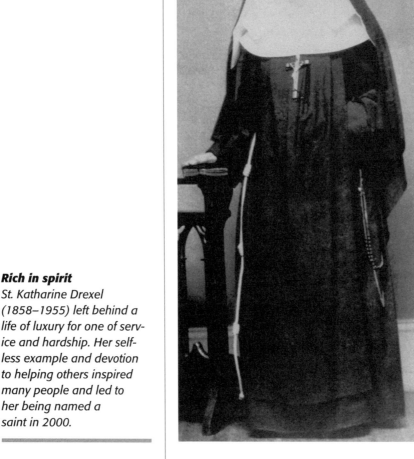

Rich in spirit
St. Katharine Drexel (1858–1955) left behind a life of luxury for one of service and hardship. Her selfless example and devotion to helping others inspired many people and led to her being named a saint in 2000.

She and her religious community did missionary work among African-Americans and Native Americans, and in 1925 founded the first university for African-Americans, Xavier University of New Orleans.

After suffering a heart attack in the 1930s, she dedicated herself to prayer and devotion to the Eucharist. She died at the age of 96 in 1955. In 1964 Philadelphia's Cardinal John Krol urged the church to investigate her cause for sainthood and in October 2000, Pope John Paul II declared her a saint in ceremony at the Vatican.

Dorothy Day (1897–1980) and the Catholic Worker

Dorothy Day was noted both for her contributions to society and for her Catholicism. She represents a radical form of living the Gospel among the poor. In 1932, Day and a Frenchman named Peter Maurin founded the Catholic Worker movement, a lay initiative designed to address the needs of the poor. The movement included a newspaper, a soup kitchen, and a shelter that has served as a model of social action for millions of Americans, Catholic and non-Catholic. Together, Day and Maurin attempted to put into action the Vatican's call for Catholics to put social justice into practice, to create places where the poor could be cared for with dignity.

Born in Brooklyn in 1897, Day was a convert to Catholicism. Already considered a saint by many Catholics, Day was suggested for the honor by Cardinal John O'Connor, the archbishop of New York from 1984 until his death in 2000. However, Day came to Catholicism with some baggage. She moved often, quit college after two years, worked as a journalist, changed jobs, was married and divorced, had an abortion, bore a baby out of wedlock, befriended the writer Eugene O'Neill—all before she found a spiritual home as a Catholic in 1927.

In 1932, Day teamed up with Maurin in New York, and together the two staunch pacifists founded a newspaper, the *Catholic Worker*. It sold for a penny a copy and grew to a circulation of 200,000 on the eve of World War II. Their motive was not profit; it was prophecy in the classical sense of the biblical prophets who called God's people to account for their actions. They also opened hospitality houses for the poor, the first one being Day's apartment. This was a simple space that eventually became overcrowded with poor people who frequented it for food and a place to sleep. The volunteers running the house assumed the poverty of the guests so that it was difficult for an outsider to tell them apart. But the idea took hold and by World War II there were houses and farms spread around the country.

Day's identification with the poor would be matched only by that of Mother Teresa, an Albanian nun who worked in India, later in the century. Her deep spirituality, as well as her unsettled youth, paralleled that of Thomas Merton, a monk 20 years her junior (see page 100). Day dedicated herself to works of mercy. While she respected the church and drew her strength form her deep Catholic faith, she never let the church interfere with her mission.

The Catholic Worker movement continues to flourish to this day, with more than 130 Houses of Hospitality throughout the United States. The members of the movement still embrace voluntary poverty and advocate for the poor as well as feed and clothe them. The newspaper maintains a circulation of 100,000 worldwide. In 1996, Paulist Films released a full-length feature film, *Entertaining Angels*, about Dorothy Day's life in which Moira Kelly played Day and Martin Sheen played Peter Maurin. Her autobiography, *The Long Loneliness*, originally published in 1952, reached a new generation in its reissue in 1997. The 100th anniversary of her birth and her candidacy for sainthood focused additional attention on her life and ministry.

Thomas Merton (1915–1968)

For much of his life Thomas Merton, arguably the most influential monk (a priest who lives away from society with other monks) in recent memory, lived the quiet life of a hermit on the grounds of Our Lady of Gethsemani Trappist monastery in Kentucky. (A monastery is a special place of residence for monks, or priests who seek to be alone to pray. The Trappists are an order of monks, much as the Jesuits are an order of priests.) That solitude disguised a whirlwind of intensity, controversy, and contribution to the American and world church. Like Dorothy Day, he had no strong attachment to religion in his youth. Born in France in 1915, he grew up in that country, as well as in England, and on Long Island, New York. In his early years. Merton was a student at Cambridge and Columbia universities. He fathered a child but did not marry, flirted with Communism, converted to Catholicism at 23, and joined the Trappists at 26. Day influenced Merton's decision to become a Catholic; he was impressed with her efforts on behalf of the poor.

Early in his monastic life he published *The Seven Storey Mountain*, a best-selling autobiography. His life as a monk was never as peaceful as his surroundings. He was never sure about his relationship with the abbot (the head of a monastery) and about the pull of the world, despite his desire for solitude. His genius was sometimes tainted with pride. With his popularity as an author and his passion for justice, he led a complicated existence, far from the simple monastic life he desired.

Merton provided a glimpse into monastic life for millions of Americans who read his books. He made the contemplative life more than respected; he made it attractive. The number of people who wanted to join increased at Gethsemani, and no doubt Merton's presence was responsible. Merton was famous, but fame was not a welcome thing in the monastery. His fame and talent made his monastic life all the more difficult; partly due to the expectations the world now had for him; partly because, even in the monastery, the side effects of fame were jealousy and envy.

Merton eventually turned his attention from the monastery to the world, involving himself in the problems of racism, war, and the environment. The monastery remained home for Merton, but he traveled regularly to confer with others of like mind and to participate in conferences. He also changed his lifestyle, retreating to a hermitage in the forest near the monastery. There he found the solitude that had eluded him in the larger community. He continued to publish scholarly works, poetry, fiction, and spiritual books. Ironically, his life ended outside of the quiet monastic world of Kentucky. He died in an accident in Bangkok, Thailand, on December 10, 1968, while attending a conference on world religions.

George Higgins (1916–2002)

One of the best known figures in the labor movement in America, Monsignor (a title honoring a priest) George Higgins was born in 1916 in Chicago and ordained for the Archdiocese of Chicago in 1940. He served on the staff of the National Catholic Welfare Conference, now known as the United States Conference of Catholic Bishops, from 1944 to 1980 and was director of their social action department, from 1954 to 1967. He later taught at the Catholic University of America in Washington, D.C.

Higgins championed human rights and economic justice, standing up for the working person. Higgins served on numerous national committees that advocated worker, civil, and human rights. He wrote a column called *The Yardstick* for the *New York Catholic* newspaper. In 2000, President Clinton gave Msgr. Higgins the Presidential Medal of Freedom, the nation's highest civilian honor. The award recognized his contribution to the American worker. His followers dubbed him the "labor priest" because of all he had done for workers. When bestowing the honor President Clinton said: "For more than 60 years now, [Higgins] has organized, marched, prayed, and bled for the social and economic justice of working Americans."

AMERICAN SAINTS

This is the list of people who have been named saints or who are being considered for sainthood ("Blessed"), and who were either born in or did most of their work in America:

SAINTS

St. Rene Goupil
(1607–1642)

St. Isaac Jogues
(1607–1646)

St. Rose Duschene
(1769–1852)

St. Elizabeth Seton
(1774–1781)

St. John Neumann
(1811–1860)

St. Frances X. Cabrini
(1850–1917)

St. Katherine Drexel
(1858–1952)

BLESSED

Kateri Tekakwitha
(1656–1680)

Fr. Juniperro Serra
(1713–1784)

Mother Guerin, S.P.
(1798–1856)

Fr. Francis X. Seelos
(1819–1867)

Fr. Damien (the Leper)
(1840–1889)

Higgins often showed up to join workers in picket lines in support of their causes, sometimes upsetting management and business owners, many of whom were Catholics themselves. His writing was equally forceful, and he was never afraid to take on the most powerful corporations and executives. Higgins died in May 2002.

Two Leaders in Education

Many Americans know the University of Notre Dame for its winning football teams and Georgetown University for its successful basketball teams. Their success in sports mirrors their overall rise to prominence among American universities. Each school ranks with the finest universities nationally and attracts students who are among the most accomplished in the nation. They stand as symbols of the rise to prominence of Catholics in the past 50 years.

Behind their success stand two visionary men, Father Theodore Hesburgh (b. 1917) of the Order of the Holy Cross, and Father Timothy Healy (1923–1992) of the Society of Jesus. Hesburgh was president of Notre Dame from 1952–1987 and Healy was Georgetown's president from 1976 to 1989.

Hesburgh was the 15th president of the University of Notre Dame. He is one of the most influential voices on higher education in America. In reviewing Hesburgh's 1990 autobiography *God, Country, and Notre Dame*, *The New York Times* wrote, "One should have to have been unconscious not to have heard of Father Hesburgh at some time during the last four decades." Born in Syracuse, New York, in 1917, he began teaching at Notre Dame and was ordained a priest in Sacred Heart Church on the campus in 1943.

After becoming the university president, Hesburgh became a national figure. He has held numerous government committee posts, dealing with civil rights, atomic energy, and third world development. As early as 1957 he was appointed a member of the U.S. Civil Rights Commission (from which he was dismissed by President Richard Nixon in 1972 after Hesburgh complained publicly of lack of progress on civil rights). He has also served on several papal commissions. President Lyndon Johnson awarded him the Medal of Freedom in 1964. He served as a director of Chase Manhattan Bank and a trustee of the Rockefeller Foundation (the first priest to be named to either), has been the recipient of more than 120 honorary degrees, and held the longest tenure of any president of an American institution of higher education. A skilled fundraiser, he improved the reputation and visibility of the University of Notre Dame nationally and internationally. The annual budget went from $9 million to $176 million, the school funds from $9 million to $350 million, and enrollment nearly doubled.

Healy entered the Society of Jesus (Jesuits) after high school. After college and several other academic jobs, he became the 46th president of Georgetown University in 1976. In 1989 he was named president of the New York Public Library, a position he held until his death in 1992. Healy came to Georgetown with the intention of making it one of America's top universities. While president of Georgetown, Healy oversaw a significant expansion of the campus, a rise in academic standing, a six-fold increase in the endowment, and an increase in minority enrollment. Healy defended American Catholic universities as places of intellectual freedom, even if some in the Church preferred they only offer official Catholic teachings in the classroom.

During his years at Georgetown, the university attracted higher caliber faculty and students, fulfilling Healy's vision. Among Georgetown's graduates are former President William J. Clinton; Supreme Court Justice Antonin Scalia; broadcast journalist Maria Shriver; Project Hope founder William Walsh; Tony-award winning writers Jack Hofsiss and John Guare; author William Peter Blatty; National Football League commissioner Paul Tagliabue; and basketball stars Patrick Ewing and Alonzo Mourning.

John F. Kennedy (1917–1963)

John Kennedy was elected as the first Catholic president of the United States in 1960. Born into a prominent Massachusetts family, Kennedy was groomed for greatness from his earliest years. He studied at Harvard University and then joined the U.S. Navy during World War II. He was in charge of a ship, PT-109, that was sunk by Japanese forces. He earned great acclaim for his heroism in helping his men recover from the attack, and later enabling them to be rescued by American forces.

After the war, he went into politics, first winning a place in the House of Representatives and then in the U.S. senate as a Democrat from Massachusetts. Kennedy was a popular and attractive and a dynamic speaker. Though his Catholic faith was seen by some as a hindrance to his political career (see page 47), he successfully overcame this perceived problem. He led the United States for three years until he was assassinated on November 22, 1963.

Daniel Berrigan (b. 1920)

Daniel Berrigan is a Jesuit priest, poet, teacher, and anti-war icon. He has lived his life pursuing justice, no matter what the personal cost. Berrigan, best known as an anti-war protester during the Vietnam War, has been a fugitive, teacher, actor, and he has often lived a life of poverty. Berrigan was once on the FBI's most wanted list. He and his brother Philip (also a priest at the time) frequently protested America's involvement in the Vietnam War by picketing in front of the Pentagon and other government facilities, often resulting in their arrest.

In May 1967, Daniel and Philip joined a small group of anti-war protesters in an act of civil disobedience that shocked many Americans, including Catholics. They entered a Selective Service office in Maryland and removed military draft records. They put them into trash cans, took them out into the parking lot, and burned them. In an explanatory letter, Daniel wrote, "Our apologies, good friends, for the fracture of good order. The burning of paper, instead of children—when will you say no to this war? The war stops here."

Both of the brothers went into hiding to avoid prison. Philip was a fugitive for 12 days, before the FBI caught him in a church. Daniel remained on the run for months before being captured. Philip served three years of his sentence and Daniel served less than two years. In 1980 they repeated their civil disobedience when they entered a factory where nose cones for warheads were made. The group hammered two nose cones, poured blood on documents, and offered prayers for peace. Known as the "Ploughshares Eight" (after the biblical text saying that swords should be turned into ploughshares), they were arrested and later convicted and sentenced to five to 10 years in jail. After a long court battle, they were paroled before they completed their sentences. Daniel Berrigan continued to write poetry, to lecture, and to protest government actions and policies he considered immoral or unjust.

Antonin Scalia (b. 1936)

A member of the U. S. Supreme Court since 1986, Antonin Scalia is a devout Catholic. He and his wife, Maureen, have nine children, one of whom is a priest in Arlington, Virginia. Born in 1936, Scalia went to

A Catholic Justice
Supreme Court Justice
Antonin Scalia, shown here
receiving an honorary
degree from Catholic
University in 2001, is one
of three Catholic Justices,
along with Anthony Kennedy
and Clarence Thomas.

Georgetown and Harvard Law School. He was a lawyer and taught at Virginia, Georgetown, Chicago, and Stanford. He was appointed by President Ronald Reagan and confirmed as Associate Justice.

He is a conservative member of the court. In talks outside the court chambers, he has spoken in defense of religious beliefs and practices and about his faith. On the court, he has advocated closer ties between the church and state, favoring clergy-led prayer at graduations, public funds for religiously affiliated school programs, and anti-abortion legislation. He was one of four votes against when the Supreme Court reaffirmed the right to abortion in 1992. He resigned from Georgetown's Board of Advisors over differences with the way the university interpreted its Catholic identity and the freedom of expression it permitted students who disagree with Catholic teachings. He, himself, however, has publicly disagreed with the church's anti-capital punishment stance.

Helen Prejean, C.S.J. (b. 1939)

Sister Helen Prejean is an internationally known opponent of the death penalty. She published an extraordinary personal account of her

Brave woman talking
Sister Helen Prejean has become one of America's most well-known opponents of the death penalty. Along with personal work with convicts, she speaks to numerous groups about her belief that capital punishment is wrong.

opposition to the death penalty in 1993 in the best-selling book *Dead Man Walking*. It has been translated into 10 languages. In 1996, the book became a successful film by the same name and Susan Sarandon won an Academy Award for her portrayal of Sister Prejean. In 2000, the book served as the basis for an opera by Jake Heggis.

Born in 1939 in Baton Rouge, Sister Prejean has worked in Louisiana all her life. She joined the Sisters of St. Joseph of Medaille in 1957 when she was 18 years old. Her religious community pledged itself to "stand on the side of the poor." Since 1982, when she began her correspondence with death-row inmate Elmo Patrick Sonnier, she has devoted her ministry to counseling death-row inmates and the families of their victims. She accompanied Sonnier to his electrocution. Since that time, she has decried the immorality of capital punishment while concurrently advocating for victims' rights.

She founded Survive, a victims' advocacy group, served as a board member and chair of the National Coalition to Abolish the Death Penalty, lectures nationwide, and was twice nominated for the Nobel Peace Prize. She continues to work to abolish the death penalty in the United States and around the world.

Martin Sheen (b. 1940)

The well known actor Martin Sheen is an active and devout Catholic who defends the poor, practices civil disobedience based on conscience, and understands Catholicism as a call to justice. Born in Ohio in 1940, Sheen (whose name at birth was Ramon Estevez) grew up in a pious Roman Catholic family. A self-described liberal Catholic, he is a social activist who has been arrested more than 50 times in his fight to gain rights for the poor, stop the build-up of nuclear weapons, and protest unjust government policies. He went to the Philippines to head an international fact-finding mission investigating the plight of the urban poor. In 1988 he fasted with Cesar Chavez (see page 30) to protest the poor working conditions and low wages of migrant farm workers. Along with a group of religious leaders, he was arrested in 1997 while supporting strawberry workers in their fight to join the United Farm Workers.

Sheen is also a participant in Greenpeace's efforts to preserve the environment. In 1995, he and Greenpeace founder Paul Watson, were beaten by seal hunters on the remote Magdelene Islands in the Gulf of St. Lawrence while trying to convince them to stop killing seals and selling their parts. He was also arrested while protesting nuclear

The arrest wing
Catholic actor Martin Sheen has long been active in social causes. Before he became the star of TV's The West Wing, *on which he plays the president of the United States, he was arrested in 1997 for taking part in a demonstration in support of farm workers in California.*

testing in Nevada. Sheen has appeared in several films dealing with Catholic figures and themes including *Entertaining Angels*, the Dorothy Day story. He plays the role of the president in the popular television drama, *The West Wing*.

Rudolph Giuliani (b. 1944)

Rudolph W. Giuliani was born in 1944 in Brooklyn, New York. He attended Bishop Loughlin Memorial High School in Brooklyn, Manhattan College in the Bronx, and New York University Law School in Manhattan, graduating *magna cum laude* in 1968. In 1970, Giuliani joined the office of the U.S. Attorney. He was appointed chief of the narcotics unit and later executive U.S. attorney. In 1975, he moved to Washington, D.C. as the associate deputy attorney general and chief of staff to the deputy attorney general. From 1977 to 1981, Giuliani practiced law in New York. In 1981, Giuliani was named associate attorney general. At the Department of Justice, Giuliani oversaw all of the U.S. Attorney Offices' federal law enforcement agencies, the Bureau of Corrections, the Drug Enforcement Agency, and the U.S. Marshals.

In 1983, Giuliani was appointed U.S. attorney for the Southern District of New York, where he was quite successful in prosecuting criminals. In 1989, Giuliani entered the race for mayor of New York City as a candidate of the Republican and Liberal parties, losing by the closest margin in city history. However, he ran again in 1993, won, and became the 107th mayor of the City of New York. He was noted for his tough stance against crime and welfare-to-work policies that helped to restore New York City to a new level of safety and financial security. He also cut taxes and balanced the budget.

He will long be remembered as a hero for his extraordinary leadership in New York after the September 11, 2001, attacks on the World Trade Center. For his efforts, and as a symbol of all in New York who contributed to the restoration of the city and the country, *Time* magazine named him Person of the Year for 2001.

Giuliani is a lifelong Catholic who, in his public life, sometimes opposed and sometimes defended the church.

Madonna (b. 1958)

Superstar singer, dancer, and actress Madonna acknowledges her Catholic upbringing in many of her songs. Born Madonna Louise Cic-

GEORGE STEPHANOPOULOS

Former Clinton White House advisor and current ABC News political commentator George Stephanopoulos, once an altar boy in the Greek Orthodox Church, is the son of a Greek Orthodox priest. In a speech at the University of Buffalo in 1999, he said: "My political beliefs are rooted in my religious principles. I think we have a duty to love one another as we love ourselves, to take responsibility for ourselves and our communities to the limits of our ability. And to never forget that we all also have responsibility to help care for those, who through no fault of their own, cannot care for themselves." In 2001 he married actress Alexandra Wentworth in a ceremony presided over by his father at the Greek Orthodox Archdiocesan Cathedral of the Holy Trinity in New York.

cone on August 16, 1958, in Bay City, Michigan, as the oldest of eight children, she was named after her mother who died when she was six years old.

Her father brought her up in a strict Catholic household, and she attended the local Catholic high school. She thought it was oppressive and recalls in a statement widely quoted on the Internet, "they would hit you across the back with a stapler if you were disobedient. I wanted to do everything everybody told me I couldn't do, I couldn't wear makeup, I couldn't wear nylons, I couldn't cut my hair, I couldn't go on dates, I couldn't even go to the movies with my friends." Although an excellent student, she disobeyed the rules whenever she could. She would roll up her uniform skirt until it was short, go into the bathroom and put make-up and nylon stockings on.

Madonna put her talent to work in the theatre department, where she had the lead part in school productions. She attended the University of Michigan for two years on a dance scholarship before seeking fame and fortune in the music industry.

Many of her videos and songs deal with Catholic themes. Never one to miss a religious pun or reference, Madonna named her 1991 greatest hits album the *Immaculate Collection*. The creation of Jesus inside his mother Mary is called the Immaculate Conception.

A Diverse Group Serving the Church and America

As these brief portraits illustrate, American Catholics have contributed to American life in a variety of ways from serving the poor to fine-tuning the conscience of the nation. However, they represent millions more who integrate their Catholic faith into their lives daily, serving God and their country.

CARSON DALY

The popular host of MTV's *Total Request Live*, Daly is well-known among America's young people. Although he spends most of his time hanging out with rock stars, Daly also tries to remain a faithful Catholic, as he has said in numerous interviews. He studied at the Jesuit college Loyola Marymount University in Los Angeles, and briefly considered becoming a priest before turning to the entertainment world. He was a popular DJ in Los Angeles before he switched to television, where he works for MTV and now also hosts a late-night interview show on ABC.

7

Catholic America: What Is Next?

THE CATHOLIC CHURCH HAS A RICH HISTORY, A VIBRANT PRESENT, and a promising future in America. The church has changed over the centuries, yet it maintains its central beliefs and practices. American Catholics, as part of a worldwide church, recognize that they must listen to the church's teachings. As Americans, they recognize equally that they have a responsibility to be good citizens. Sometimes, especially on moral matters, loyalty to their church and their country can conflict. However, it is entirely possible to be American and Catholic.

The church today is very different from the one the early settlers knew, and it differs from the one that Bishop John Carroll presided over in America. The church in the 21st century is bigger, more ethnically diverse, and wealthier than in its past. It takes its place in a more religiously diverse nation, and its followers blend in more than they ever have in the past. It faces new and different challenges and has the resources to face those challenges.

Fewer Priests and Nuns

The church faces the challenge of declining numbers of nuns and priests. Since Vatican II the American church has seen a drop in vocations. This has affected the sisterhood particularly. In the mid-1960s there were approximately

180,000 nuns in America. Today there is half that number and the average age is 70 years old. Sisters have played a key role in the development of American Catholicism in education, health care, social ministries, and parish work. Some contemplative orders (living quiet lives devoted to prayer) have attracted vocations, but the majority of religious orders are facing severe shortages of personnel.

The number of priests has also declined in the past 40 years from about 58,000 in the 1960s to approximately 47,000 today. These declines in nuns and priests have occurred while the Catholic population has risen 34 percent since the 1960s. Dioceses across the country have had to combine or close parishes because of a lack of priests, while others are parishes with no resident priest. Women's religious orders have trimmed their work and can no longer staff schools as they did in the past. Their aging population means that some convents (houses for nuns) have become virtual nursing homes for elderly sisters.

However, one positive consequence of this has been that the laity has taken on greater responsibility for the Church. Lay people staff parishes as professionals, and hundreds more volunteer in each parish.

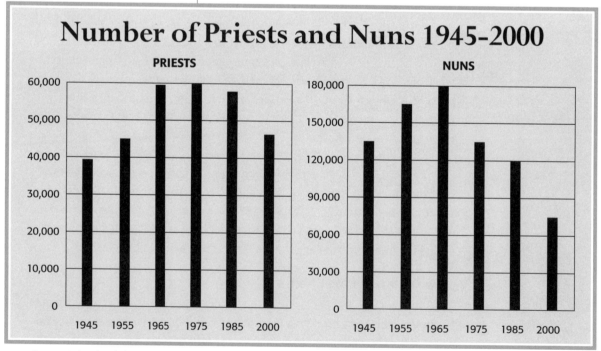

Number of Priests and Nuns 1945-2000

Source: National Catholic Report

Center of the storm
Boston's Cardinal Bernard Law was the focus of a major scandal that erupted in 2002. Law and other church leaders were accused of not fully reporting sexual offenses of their priests against young people. The scandal drew new attention to the role of Catholic leaders and the church's place in American society.

Increasingly, the church trusts them with managing property, directing programs, and even with direct ministry. They assume the responsibility for the church that their baptism invites them and entitles them to do. They work with pastors, nuns, and fellow laypeople. The needs of the church continue to be met, but no longer exclusively by priests and nuns. In 1950, 17,000 lay people worked full-time for the church; by 2000 that number had grown to 180,000. Lay influence grows daily and it is bound to have a long-term impact.

Scandals Put the Church Under Pressure

In 2002, a scandal rocked the Archdiocese of Boston and the entire American Catholic Church. During the trial of a priest for pedophilia (sexual abuse of a child, which is a major crime), the *Boston Globe* looked into the Archdiocese of Boston's handling of other cases in which priests molested children. They discovered that Cardinal Bernard Law had reassigned the priest on trial, as well as others, to other parishes, and that he had done so even after the Church knew that the priests had committed crimes involving children. The priests received therapy, and were thought to be healed, but some repeated their criminal activity. Boston, and other dioceses around the country, created new policies to prevent such terrible tragedies in the future. Victims of the abuse sued the dioceses and the Church paid out hundreds of millions of dollars to settle lawsuits.

Across the country many other victims of abuse came forward even after years of silent suffering. They went to therapists, lawyers, district attorneys, and newspapers. The press covered the incidents extensively. The negative publicity was devastating to the image of the church, and the lawsuits were financially draining. Settling out of court, which the church generally preferred to avoid further public embarrassment, cost millions of dollars. Some dioceses teetered on the edge of insolvency.

The priesthood was deeply hurt by these cases. Although the accused priests represented a small fraction of the clergy, the fact that priests were involved shocked and disappointed many Catholics and non-Catholics alike. Priests who had no involvement in the scandals found themselves lumped together with priests facing or convicted of criminal charges. The fact that the church had denied or covered up numerous cases for years made many people very angry. The image of the church as a place of refuge and a place of safety was terribly hurt. The result of the ongoing scandal may not be known fully for years.

One thing that did result from the publicity and the pressure from Catholics was that the American church began to examine some of its long held practices. People began to question such traditional things as requiring that priests remain celibate and even to suggest that women be considered for the priesthood. Of course, the church in America does not have the authority to change the regulations and disciplines of the church. Only the Vatican can make such changes.

The Changing Composition of the Church

As the American church grows, it changes. The church in the year 2000 looks quite different from the church of 1700, 1800, or 1900. The church of 2100 will look different from today's church. Immigrants from England, Ireland, Italy, Germany, Poland, France, Spain, and other European countries built the American church. Immigrants from Latin America, Asia, India, and Africa will build on that foundation. The church functions best when it welcomes the stranger and provides a spiritual identity to those who enjoy the privilege of citizenship in the United States. The composition of the church changes with every generation, but it remains the Body of Christ.

Hispanic Catholics

The Church in America continues to grow, with more than 65 million followers today. The face of the church in the 21st century, not unlike the 19th and 20th centuries, will be ethnically diverse. The rising number of Hispanic members of the Church in the United States will demand increasing attention. The birth rate among the Hispanic community is higher than the national average and the vast majority of Hispanics are Catholic, so they account for most of the growth of the Church. There are more than 25 million Americans of Hispanic origin.

Estimates of how much of this large and growing community identifies itself as Catholic range from 60 to 80 percent. Conservative estimates place the Hispanic Catholic population in America at about 15 million, making them about one-fourth of the U.S. Catholic population. About 60 percent of U.S. Hispanics come from Mexico, 13 percent from Puerto Rico, 5 percent from Cuba, and 8 percent from a collection of other countries.

Latinos clearly differ from one another in background, style and preferences. The Hispanic community differs from the majority of Catholics in a number of ways, too. Many who have recently immigrated do not speak English well and are learning the language and customs of the country. By and large, Hispanics represent an undereducated population in which less than 10 percent have graduated from college and high school dropout rates remain as high as 40 percent. Their spiritual needs, arising from a faith that revolves around religious devotion and tradition, rather than doctrines and Church pronouncements, often go unmet. In many ways, their religious habits hearken back to the Catholicism of the Anglo population in the 1950s, favoring religious medals around their necks, statues in their homes, and family prayer.

HELP FROM THE PEOPLE

Increasingly, the laity is taking responsibility within the church. In 1950, 17,000 lay people worked full-time for the Catholic Church; by 2000 that number grew to over 180,000. Lay influence grows daily and it is bound to have a long-term impact. The face of Catholicism will be different as the 21st century progresses.

One of the major differences is the make-up of local leadership. A result of the priest shortage, brought on at least in part by Vatican's views on women's ordination and married clergy, is that laypeople are assuming greater responsibility for day-to-day operations and ministry. Tasks previously reserved to the clergy and nuns, such as pastoral counseling, religious education, youth ministry, sacramental preparation, hospital ministry, pastoral administration, and liturgical planning, are sometimes now handled by lay professionals, volunteers, or a combination of both.

One result of the Church's lack of attention to their spiritual needs is that between 1980 and 1990 5 million Hispanic Catholics left the Catholic Church. Some reports indicate that Hispanics leave the Church at the rate of about 100,000 a year. They often move to Evangelical or Pentecostal churches where they are more likely to find a form of worship and spirituality that suits their penchant for popular religion—a place where the theology is simpler, the ritual more exciting, and the emotional quotient high.

The church encourages vocations among the Hispanic community but, as in other ethnic groups, the response is often not enough. In places where there is a large Hispanic population , such as California, dioceses require that all priests learn Spanish. In other areas, the community seeks out Spanish-speaking clergy and some dioceses designate particular parishes or centers with bilingual staff to serve them.

Will the future fill it?
The Shrine of the Immaculate Conception in Washington D.C. is the central Catholic churches in the United States. As the American church grows and changes in the 21st century, what will the faithful who will fill this church look like?

But they are also the future, or at least a big part of it. The church therefore attempts to serve them better, recognize them more, and encourage them to take part as leaders. The church cannot afford to ignore them, underserve them, or otherwise disregard their concerns. It needs to integrate Hispanics while at the same time it must respect their language, cultures, and religious practices. They represent a significant part of the Church at present and a growing presence in the future.

Another group that is growing within the Church comes from Asia, especially Vietnam and the Philippines. These countries have long had large Catholic populations. Recent Asian immigrants bring elements of their culture to the American Church that enhances its richness and diversity.

Issues of Authority

Part of the decline of the Catholic subculture in the second half of the 20th century came from Catholics' changing attitude towards church authority. Vincent of Lerins, a fifth century monk and saint, defined "orthodox" faith as that which has been believed "always, everywhere, and by all the faithful." Such a definition would be difficult to support in today's American church. Many beliefs and practices are not held equally by all the faithful everywhere. The Roman Catholic Church in America today has a diversity unequaled in its history. At the beginning of the third millennium, American Catholics no longer "pay, pray, and obey" the way their ancestors readily did. Unlike their grandparents, who generally held church authority as total, today's Catholics more readily disagree with church authorities. The scandals of 2002 may have increased that level of disagreement and discord. The church remains important in the lives of many Catholics, but it must compete for their attention and allegiance with social, cultural, and economic forces that pull them in different directions.

The areas in which the church carries significant authority in a believer's life are fewer than in the past, and the authority is of a different type. This is due, in part, to the fact that American Catholics are (by and large) no longer an immigrant community; also, that the educational levels of American Catholics today are much higher overall than 100 years ago. Their economic status is greater. Disagreeing is not as bad as it was once thought to be.

The Church and the Future

The fact that the church faces significant challenges on a number of fronts does not mean that it is in danger of dying, collapsing, or disappearing. Some of the problems that the Roman Catholic Church in America faces can be overcome with greater effort, more sensitivity, and clear vision. Others appear beyond its immediate control. This is due, in part, to its ties to Rome, which prevent it from embarking on national initiatives that conflict with the Vatican's agenda, and in part to an American culture that shapes Catholics in the same way that it shapes other citizens. A number of American cultural forces work against the Church's agenda, forcing Catholics to resist or oppose elements of culture that society as a whole accepts. Of course, Catholics do not always do so.

The church can, however, shape its response to culture, inform its members, offer alternatives where possible, and provide reasons to resist cultural pressures when necessary. No one can reasonably expect all Catholics to think alike, just as no one can expect all Americans to agree on federal or local issues. The church is accustomed to differing views among its membership. On those issues in which some make errors, there is forgiveness. On matters on which they disagree, there remains disagreement. In either case, the official church usually approaches change cautiously and creates it slowly.

Conclusion

In the past 40 years America has witnessed the erosion of a Catholic culture that supported and defined Catholics. Neighbors do not define themselves primarily by their religion as their immigrant ancestors did. In some urban settings, apartment dwellers do not even know their neighbors' names, much less their religious persuasions. Neighborhoods are more likely to group together in similar economic classes rather than because they are Catholics, Protestants, Muslims, or Jews. In the sprawling suburbs, most people do not notice if their neighbor's garage door goes up on Sunday morning. And if it does, it may be to permit someone to retrieve the Sunday paper or to drive to pick up Grandma for brunch instead of to go to church. This fact, which many Catholics regret, signifies the merging of Catholics into the wider American culture, just as Protestants and Jews before them, and now Muslims, Hindus, and Buddhists after them.

THE CHURCH AND YOUNG PEOPLE

The Church does its best to attract and serve the needs of young people. One strategy to attract them involves the Vatican. Since 1984 the Vatican has sponsored an event called World Youth Day staged in different countries. World Youth Days began with Pope John II inviting all young people to Rome in 1984 for prayer and celebration. Other gatherings have taken place around the world since then. In 1993 it was held in Denver, Colorado and the pope attended.

World Youth Day is a week-long chance for people ages 16–35 from all over the globe to come together to share their faith and experience with the world. The week includes prayer, song, concerts, drama, community building, and camaraderie.

Much of the tension over identity in the American church has to do with American society and culture (to which Catholics contribute and by which they are affected). Americans are democratic; Catholicism is not. Americans often follow or even set trends. The church is not trendy. Americans live in a pluralistic society that values tolerance for many views and practices, whereas the church holds moral positions that do not abide tolerance. Americans live in an affluent, developed, and materialist country. The church spreads a Gospel that identifies with the poor. Americans prize their independence. The church "takes care of" her faithful. Often Americans are asked to compete and win at work. The church asks them to form a community of forgiveness and compassion. Americans demand reasonable answers to difficult questions from their political leaders. The church asks them to accept some things on faith alone or on the authority of the church.

It is no wonder that American Catholics sometimes find it difficult to be both. What their culture says is good, their church sometimes says is not.

Catholics in America differ from previous generations in that they are not subject to suspicion or exclusion solely because of their Catholicism. Some will adopt the patterns of the larger culture; others will resist. In either case, they represent a big part of American society and popular culture that cannot be ignored.

GLOSSARY

annulment The only official way that the Catholic Church approves the end of a marriage.

archdiocese The main diocese in a regional group of dioceses; led by an archbishop.

baptism One of the sacraments; water is poured over the candidate's head and the words "I baptize you in the name of the Father, the Son, and the Holy Spirit" are recited. The candidate becomes a Catholic Christian.

bioethics The study of the morality or ethics of medical procedures.

bishop Priest promoted to lead a diocese.

cardinal Appointed by the pope to act in an advisory role in governing the church. The archbishop of major U.S. dioceses are usually promoted to cardinal.

censorship The act of preventing, or trying to prevent, the publication or distribution of material that a group believes to be objectionable.

communion receiving bread and wine in the Eucharist.

confirmation A sacrament of initiation usually received during teenage years, after a person has been baptized and received communion. The rite signals a person's acceptance of the faith.

convent A group residence for nuns.

council Official gathering of bishops with the pope to establish beliefs and practices for the entire Catholic Church.

creed An authorized code of beliefs.

deacon An ordained minister just below a priest in rank. Those who are becoming priests first receive this order. Others receive it to become permanent deacons.

diocese The geographic region that a bishop is in charge of. A diocese is made up of a number of parishes.

disciple An early follower of Jesus.

encyclical A document issued by the pope and addressed to the entire church worldwide.

Eucharist Means "thanksgiving," another word for the mass and for the sacrament in which bread and wine is turned into the body and blood of Jesus.

Evangelical Promoting a type of Christianity that is very concerned with spreading the Gospel and convincing others to become Christians.

Gospel Means "good news," and is the term used for the four accounts of Jesus' life and activities written by Mark, Matthew, Luke, and John.

Holy Orders The sacrament through which a man becomes a deacon, priest, or bishop.

imprimatur Latin for "let it be printed," the term is used in Catholic books that have been approved by a bishop as being in agreement with church teaching.

liturgy The official public prayers and rites of the church.

mass The celebration of the Eucharist, presided over by a priest and in which laypeople take part.

mission Church set up in a place where there has never been a church before.

monastery Group residence for monks.

nihil obstat Means "nothing stands in the way," and means approval of a book by a theological censor before being approved by a bishop.

ordination A sacrament that makes a person a deacon, priest, or bishop. Also known as Holy Orders.

orthodox A branch of Christianity that follows some of the rites of the Catholic Church, but for the most part does not answer to the authority of the pope.

parish The members of a local church community that worship in a designated church building; the main organizational unit of Catholic laypeople.

pastor A priest in charge of a parish.

pastoral letter An official document issued by an individual bishop or group of bishops addressed to the people in the region which they oversee.

pope The title for the head of the Roman Catholic Church.

priest A man ordained by a bishop to perform sacraments and other ministries. His title is "Father."

Protestant A Christian who belongs to a community with roots in the 16th-century Reformation when some Christians broke their ties with Rome.

Reconciliation A sacrament in which a person asks God, through a priest, to forgive him or her for sins. Also known as Confession.

Resurrection The event in which Christians believe that Jesus rose from the dead three days after his crucifixion.

sacrament One of seven central rites or ceremonies that connect the faithful to God, Christ, and the Holy Spirit. The sacraments are Baptism, Eucharist, Confirmation, Reconciliation (Confession), Matrimony, Anointing of the Sick, and Holy Orders (Ordination).

scripture The texts of the Bible.

sisters A collective name for most nuns; also used as a title, e.g. Sister Mary Grace.

TIME LINE

1634	First Catholics arrive in America in Maryland.
1790	John Carroll becomes first American bishop.
1798	Pope Pius VI establishes Baltimore as the first Catholic diocese in America.
1830s	First wave of Catholic immigrants begins arriving from Europe.
1893	Pope Leo XIII issues letter warning Americans not to think of their church as separate from Roman Catholic Church.
1919	National Catholic Welfare Council formed, becoming first official organization of American bishops.
1928	Catholic Governor Al Smith of New York is defeated in run for president.
1933	Catholic Worker movement founded.
1960	John F. Kennedy is elected first Catholic president of the United States.
1962–65	Second Vatican Council meets and proposes sweeping changes in Catholic life in America and around the world.
1965	Following repeal of some immigration laws, wave of Catholic immigrants from Asia and Latin America begins.
1973	Supreme Court rules abortion is legal, in *Roe* vs. *Wade* decision.
1979	Pope John Paul II makes first of his five trips to the United States.
1984	The United States and the Vatican establish formal diplomatic relations for the first time.
2002	The church faces a crisis of confidence when the public learns that a number of priests have sexually abused children and that bishops have covered up the crimes.

RESOURCES

Reading List

Becket, Sister Wendy, *Sister Wendy's Book of Saints.* New Orleans: Loyola Press, 1998.

Brown, Stephen F. and Khaled Anstosios, *Catholicism & Orthodox Christianity (World Religions Series).* New York: Facts On File, 2002.

Fisher, James. T., *Communion of Immigrants: A History of Catholics in America.* New York: Oxford University Press, 2002.

_____, *Catholics in America.* New York: Oxford University Press, 2000

O'Grady, Jim; Lisa Peet (illustrator), *Dorothy Day: With Love for the Poor.* New York: Ward Hill Press, 1993

Parsons, Richard D., *Valuing Sexuality: A Guide for Catholic Teens*; San Diego: Harcourt, 2002

Singer-Towns, Brian (editor); Michael O'Neill McGrath (illustrator), *The Catholic Youth Bible: New Revised Standard Version: Catholic Edition.* Winona, Minn.: St. Mary's Press 2002

Thomas, Dwayne, Michael Savelesky, *Catholics Believe.* San Diego: Harcourt, 2000

Resources on the Web

Catholic Encyclopedia Online
www.newadvent.org/cathen
An alphabetical listing of thousands of terms, people, places, and concepts important to the study of Catholics both in America and worldwide.

Catholic News Service
www.catholicnews.com
The Washington D.C.-based national information service for news relating to Catholic concerns.

Catholic Worker Movement
www.catholicworker.org
Information about Catholic Worker "hospitality houses" around the country.

Catholic Net (Spanish version)
www.es.catholic.net
Spanish-language version of national Catholic information service.

National Catholic Reporter
www.ncr.org
Web site of national Catholic newspaper.

Orthodox Church in America
www.oca.org
Information about Orthodox Christian Churches in America, a religion closely related to Catholicism.

United States Conference of Catholic Bishops
www.nccbuscc.org
News and views from the organization of American bishops.

The Vatican
www.vatican.va
Multi-language home page of the Vatican, home of the pope and world headquarters of the Roman Catholic Church.

INDEX

Note: *Italic* page numbers refer to illustrations; *t* indicates a table; and *f* indicates a figure.

abortion, 51, 69, *76,* 78, 88
absolution. *See* Eucharist; forgiveness of sins
abstinence, 75, 77
Advent, 36
Africa, 90
African-American Catholics, 32–35
  bishop, 34, 35, *90*
  protection of rights, 91
  racist groups against, 24
  slavery, 21, 96
  social organizations, 91
  and St. Katharine Drexel, 97–98
  treatment by Irish immigrants, 22
AIDS prevention, 77
Alaska, 20
America, 61
American Requiem, An, 66
Angelica, Mother, 62, *63*
anointing of the sick, 12
Anti-Defamation League, 91
apostles, 8, 11
archbishop, 16, 17, 29
architecture, *6–7,* 25
art, 12, 86
ascension, 9, 10
Asian Catholics, 36–37, 117
Atticus, 66

baptism as holy sacrament, 12, 14
Baptists, 15, 86
Baron, Rev. William R., 32
basketball teams, 56
beliefs
  author's talent to express, 66, 67
  Catholic creed, 10
  issues of authority, 117
  refinement, 12, 14
  unique to Catholicism, 13
Bells of St. Mary's, The, 59
Berrigan, Daniel, 103–104
Berrigan, Philip, 103–104
Bible
  The Gospels, 11, 67, 92, 93
  New Testament, 9
  Old Testament, 9
  use in taking oath of office, 13
bioethics, 79–80
birth control, 76–77

bishops
  African-American, 34, 35, *90*
  America's first, *19,* 95–96
  appointment by the Vatican, 21
  holy orders, 12
  on immigrants, 89
  Irish, 22
  pro-life activities, 79, 80, 89
  in Protestantism, 14
  responsibilities, 11, 16, 17, 23, 28–29, 54, 61, 96
  of Rome. *See* pope
  and slavery, 21, 96
  speaking out on social issues, 70, 71
Bishop Sheen Program, The, 62
Blatty, William Peter, 103
Blessed Americans, 101*t*
Blum, Virgil C., 91
Boggs, Lindy, 88
books, 61, 66, 67
Boston College, 56
bread and wine. *See* Eucharist
Brennen, William J., 86
Buddhism, 83
Bush, Pres. George W., 48–49, 80

Cabrini, Saint Frances X., 101*t*
calendar, 7
California, 28, 37*t,* 39–40
Calvert family, 20
Calvin, John, 14
Cambodia, 37
Canada, 19, 23
candles, 28
Cantwell, John (bishop of Los Angeles), 56
capital punishment, 51, *68–69,* 69, 70, 85, 104–105, 107
cardinals, 13, 17
Carroll, Daniel, 21
Carroll, James, 66
Carroll, John (bishop of Baltimore), *19,* 20–21, 95–96
cathedrals, 12
Catholic Broadcasters Association, 63
Catholic Charities, 82–83, 90–91
Catholic Hour, The, 62

Catholicism
  cultural influences, 44, 67, 117–119
  development of American, 19–23, 27–28
  and the future, 111–119
  migrant worker aid, 29, 105
  role of saints, 17
  vs. Protestantism, 14
Catholic League for Religious and Civil Rights, 91
Catholic News Service, 61
Catholic Online, 64
Catholic Relief Services (CRS), 30, 82
Catholics
  celebrities, 37, 100, 103
  number in the U.S., 23
  number in top ten states, 37*t*
  number of Hispanic, 115
  number worldwide, 7
  percent African-American, 34
  percent of U.S. population, 37
Catholic schools, *52–53, 53–55, 55*
  decline in students, 67
  in early America, 96
  open to African-Americans, 33, 97–98
  as part of the community, 36
  training in social action, 91–92
  voucher system for, 87
Catholic University of America, 101
Catholic Worker Movement, 96, 99–100
Catholic Youth Organization, 25
Celebration, 61
celebrities who are Catholic, 37, 100, 103
censorship, 56, 57, 58, 59
charism, 54
charities, 82–83, 90–91
Chase Manhattan Bank, 103
Chavez, Caesar, 30, *31,* 105
Chopin, Kate, 66
Christian Brothers, 54
Christmas, 11
Christopher, Warren, 87–88
Cicone, Madonna Louise. *See* Madonna

Civil War, 42, 97
Clement XIV, 95
Clinton, Pres. Bill, 80, 87, 101–102, 103, 108
Commonweal, 61
Communion. *See* Eucharist
community life, 23–25, 35–36, 44, 54, 72, 92
Community of the Holy Family
Confederacy of Dunces, A, 66
Confession, 12, 15
confirmation, 12
Constantine, 11–12
consumerism, 51
Coughlin, Father Charles E., 62–63
Council of Chalcedon, 12
Council of Constantinople, 10
Council of Nicea, 10, 12
creed, 10
crucifixion of Jesus, 8, 10, 13
Cubans, 30, 115
cultural aspects, 44, 67, 117–119
Cuomo, Mario, 79
Cursillo movement, 30

Daly, Carson, 109
Damien, Father (the Leper), 101*t*
Daschle, Sen. Tom, 88
Davis, Brother Joseph M., 34
Davis, Gov. Gray, 88
Day, Dorothy, *94–95,* 99–100, 106
deacon, 12, 16, 17, 74
Dead Man Walking, 104
death penalty. *See* capital punishment
Declaration of Independence, 21
DePaul University, 56
diocese
    charities, 82–83
    and decline in priests, 112
    definition, 16
    the oldest U.S., 19
divorce, 74
Dougherty, Dennis (cardinal of Philadelphia), 56
Dubus, Andre, 66
Duschene, Saint Rose, 101*t*

Easter, 8
Eastern division, 15
economic justice, 70–72, 89, 92, 99–100, 101–102
education. *See* Catholic schools
educational videos, 77
Entertaining Angels, 100, 106
Episcopalians, 14
epistles, 9
Estevez, Ramon. *See* Sheen, Martin

Eternal Word Television Network (EWTN), 62, 63
Eucharist
    as holy sacrament, 12, 14–15, *16*
    with Vatican II, 46
evangelical Christianity, 11, 79, 115–116

Ferraro, Geraldine, 79
Filipino Catholics, 37, 117
films. *See* movies
Fitzgerald, F. Scott, 66
Florida, 19, 30, 31, 37*t*
Flutie, Doug, 56
Flynn, Raymond, 87–88
football teams, 56
Fordham University, 56
forgiveness of sins
    mankind and the crucifixion, 8, 13
    the role of the Eucharist, 15
Franciscans, 19, 39, *94*
Francis of Assisi, Saint, 30, 39
Freeman, Mary Wilkins, 66

genetic engineering, 79–80
Georgetown University, 56, 102, 103, 106
G.I. Bill, 44
Girzone, Joseph, 67
Giuliani, Rudolph W., 86–87, *87,* 108–109
God
    authority to forgive sins, 8, 15
    authority to give/take a life, 70, 76, 79, 80
    Jesus as both God and man, 12, 13
Godspell, 59
Going My Way, 58, 59
Gonzaga University, 56
Gospel, 11, 67, 92, 93
Goupil, Saint Rene, 101*t*
Graham, Billy, 62
Greek Orthodox Church, 25, 108
Greeley, Andrew, 67
Greenpeace, 105
Gregory, Wilton (bishop of Belleville), 35, *90*
Guare, John, 103
Guerin, Mother S. P., 101*t*

Hansen, Ron, 66
Harkin, Sen. Tom, 88
Hawthorne, Nathaniel, 66
Hayes, Diana, 34
Healey, Father Timothy, 102–103
healing, 8
health care, 80–81

heretics, 12
Hesburgh, Father Theodore, 102–103
Higgins, Msgr. George, 101–102
Hijuelos, Oscar, 66
Hinduism, 83
Hispanic Catholics, 23, 28–32, 115–117
historical background
    church influence, 12–13
    Civil War, 42, 97
    early America, 19–21, 95–96
    early church, 9, 11–12, 96
    immigrant communities. *See* immigrants
    Protestant Reformation, 14
Hmong Catholics, 37
Hofsiss, Jack, 103
Holy Name Society, 25
holy orders, 12
Holy Spirit, 12
homosexuality, 69, 77–78
Houses of Hospitality, 99–100
Hughes, John J. (archbishop of New York), 42, 96–97
human rights, 50, 71, 89, 91, 101–102

Illinois, 37*t,* 101
Immaculate Conception, 13, 108
immigrants
    Asian, 36–37
    in Catholic schools, 54
    changing composition of the Church, 114–117
    Church position on, 89
    Cuban, 30
    Hispanic, 23, 28–32, 105, 115
    Irish, 21–22, 42
    Puerto Rican, 30
    south, central and eastern European, 25
    and voting, 88
intellectual freedom, 103
International Catholic Association for Radio and Television, 63
Internet
    Catholic sites, 55, 60, 64–65
    cultural effects, 57, 67
    the Pope on the, 65
    Vatican site, *64,* 64–65
Irish Catholics, 21–22, 42
Ironweed, 66
Isaiah, 8
Islam, 13, 83
Israel, 7

Jeremiah, 8

Jesuits
    Daniel Berrigan, 103–104
    early, 19, 20
    role in education, 54
    and slavery, 21
    suppression in 1773, 95
    Timothy Healey, 102, 103
Jesus Christ
    as both God and man, 12, 13
    crucifixion and resurrection, 8,
        10, 13
    Immaculate Conception, 13, 108
    of Judaism, 7
    Last Supper, 16
    Madonna and Child stamp, 11
    as the Messiah, 7, 11
    teachings, 7–8
    "What would Jesus do?", 67
Jesus Christ Superstar, 59
Jesus of Nazareth, 59
Jogues, Saint Isaac, 101t
John II, 118
John Paul II, 49, 49–51, 64, 65
    on ambassador to the Vatican,
        87
    on the death penalty, 70
    on human rights, 50, 71
    sainthood of Katharine Drexel,
        99
Johnson, Pres. Lyndon B., 102
John the Apostle, Saint, 8, 11
John XXIII, 45
Josephite Fathers and Brothers,
    21
Judaism, 7–8, 9, 13, 83, 91
Judas the Apostle, 8

Katharine Drexel, Saint, 97–99, 98
Kelly, Moira, 100
Kennedy, Anthony, 88, 107
Kennedy, Pres. John F., 47–49,
    84–85, 86
Kennedy, Sen. Edward, 79, 88
Kennedy, William, 66
Kentucky, 100, 101
Kerouac, Jack, 66
Kerry, Sen. John, 88
King, Martin Luther, Jr., 33
Knights of Columbus, 25
Korea, 36
Krol, John (cardinal of
    Philadelphia), 98

laity, 16, 112–113, 115
Last Supper, 16
Last Temptation of Christ, The, 59
Latin phrases, 46
Law, Bernard (cardinal of
    Boston), 113, 114

Legion of Decency, 56–57
Lent, 36
Leo XIII, 27–28, 71
Le Propagateur Catholique, 60
Life on the Rock, 62
Life Worth Living, 62
literature, 61, 66
living together before marriage,
    74
lobbying efforts, 85, 89–91
Long Loneliness, The, 100
Lucey, Robert E., 28, 29
Luke the Apostle, Saint, 11
Luther, Martin, 14
Lutherans, 14, 15

Madonna, 107–108
magazines, 61
Mahoney, Roger (cardinal of Los
    Angeles), 30, 65
Mambo Kings Play Songs of Love,
    The, 66
March for Life, 79
Mark the Apostle, Saint, 9, 11
Marquette University, 56
marriage
    annulment, 74–75
    and divorce, 74
    and homosexuality, 78
    "mixed," 36
    in orthodox Christianity, 25
    the sacrament of, 12, 73–74
Mary, Mother of God
    feast day, 17
    Immaculate Conception of
        Jesus, 13, 108
    Madonna and Child stamp, 11
    role in Catholicism, 13, 17
    role in Protestantism, 14
Maryland, 20–21, 54, 95
Mass
    in Latin, 46
    and the sacraments, 14, 15–16
    schedule, 15
    in Spanish, 28, 30–31
Massachusetts, 37t
Matthew the Apostle, Saint, 11
Maurin, Peter, 99
McDermott, Alice, 66
Merton, Thomas, 99, 100–101
Messiah, 7, 11
Methodists, 14, 15
Mexico, 28, 115
Micah, 8
Michigan, 37t
migrant workers, 29–30, 105
Migration and Refugee Services,
    89
missionaries, 19, 39, 40–41

missions, 39, 40, 41
Mohandas Ghandi, 30
monastic life, 100, 101
monk, 17, 100
monsignor, definition, 17, 101
Morris, Robert, 96
"Mother Angelica Live," 62
Mother Superior, definition, 17
Mourning, Alonzo, 103
Moviegoer, The, 66
movies, 55–59, 67, 100
Mundelein, George William
    (cardinal of Chicago), 63
Murray, Sen. Patty, 88
music, 28, 34, 46

Napoleon, 97
Nast, Thomas, 26
National Association for the
    Advancement of Colored
    People (NAACP), 91
National Catholic Office for
    Motion Pictures, 57
National Catholic Reporter, 60–61
National Catholic War Council,
    42–43
National Catholic Welfare
    Conference, 43, 101
National Coalition to Abolish the
    Death Penalty, 105
National Conference of Catholic
    Bishops, 43, 60
National Council of Catholic
    Women, 25
National Council of Churches of
    Christ, 25
National Office for Black
    Catholics, 34
National Office for Catholic
    Migrants, 30
National Shrine of the
    Immaculate Conception, 35
Native Americans, 19, 39, 40–41, 96,
    97–98
Neumann, Saint John, 101t
New Jersey, 37t, 55
newspapers, 60–61, 67, 96, 99, 101
New Testament of the Bible, 9
New York, 30, 37t, 41–42, 96–97,
    108–109
Nicene Creed, 10, 11
Nixon, Pres. Richard Milhouse,
    102
nuclear weapons, 72, 73, 105, 106
nuns
    administration of parishes, 16
    clothing, 46, 52–53
    decline in, 55, 111–113, 112f
    definition, 16, 17

early American, 20
  health care activities, 80–81
  number in U.S., 112
  and slavery, 21
  as teachers, *52–53*, 54

O'Connor, Flannery, 66
O'Connor, John (cardinal of New
    York), 72, 99
Ohio, 37*t*
Old Testament of the Bible, 9
Operation Rice Bowl, 82
Order of the Holy Cross, 102
organization of the Catholic
    Church, 11, 12, 43
Orthodox Catholicism
  in colonial America, 20
  creation, 15
  Greek, 25, 108
  influence of immigrants, 25
  Russian, 20, 25
  Serbian, 25
Our Mother Africa chapel, *33, 35*
Our Sunday Visitor, 61

parables, 8
parishes
  charity activities, 82
  city, 35–36
  closing, 112
  Internet sites, 65
  Irish-Catholic, 22
  "national," 23, 32
  number, 1945-2000, 36*t*
  organization, 16
  school program, 54
  with Vatican II, 46, 47
Pataki, Gov. George, 88
Paul the Apostle, Saint, 9, *9*
Paul VI, 76
Pax Christi, 92–93, *93*
Pelosi, Rep. Nancy, 88
Penance. *See* Confession
Penn, William, 20
Pennsylvania, 20, 37*t*, 92, 97
Pentecostal Church, 116
Percy, Walker, 66
Peter the Apostle, Saint, 11, 17
Pharisees, 9
Philippines, 37, 117
"Pillars of Faith," 62
Pius VI, 96
Pius IX, 71
Pius X, 28
"Ploughshares Eight," 104
political aspects, 85–93
  Catholic League for Religious
      and Civil Rights, 91
  Catholics in government, 88

Catholic vote for President, 89*t*
discrimination against
    Catholic politicians, 47, 48,
    85, 86
fall of Communism, 25
lobbying, 85, 89–91
migrant workers, 30, 105
party affiliation, 88, 89, 89*t*
religion and the Presidency,
    47–49, 85, 86, 89*t*
segregation laws, 32
separation of church and state,
    27
slavery, 21, 96
social action, 91–93
Pontius Pilate, 10
Pope. *See also* Vatican; Vatican II
  role and responsibilities, 11, 14,
      17
  roles in orthodox Christianity,
      25
poverty, 22, 70–72, 82–83, 90, 99–100
practices
  creation of rules, 11
  refinement of rules, 12, 14
prayer, 16–17
  anointing of the sick, 12
  for peace, 92–93, 104
  rosary beads, 16–17, 28
  to take oath of office, 13
  in U.S. Congress, 24
Praying, 61
Prejean, Sister Helen, C.S.J.,
    104–105
prejudice. *See* racial discrimina-
    tion; religious discrimination
pre-marital sex, 75
Presbyterians, 14, 15
Priest, The, 59
priests
  decline in, 16, 55, 111–113, 112*f*
  definition, 17
  of early America, 19, 96
  of early Christianity, 11
  health care activities, 81
  holy orders to become, 12
  immigrant, 22, 23, 29
  number African-American, 34
  in orthodox Christianity, 25
  in Protestantism, 14
  role and responsibilities, 15
  sexual offenses, 113–114
  as "witness" to marriage, 74
processions, 35
Production Code Administration,
    56–57
Project Hope, 103
Protestant Reformation, 14, 15
Protestants

discrimination against
    Catholics, 24, 53
  European colonists, 19–20
  and Hispanic immigrants, 29,
      30
  Reformation movement, 14
publishers, 60–61
Puerto Rican Catholics, 30
Puerto Rico, 19
Puritans, 20, 66

Quakers, 20
Quigley, Martin, St., 56

racial discrimination, 32–34, 89
radio, 62–64
Reagan, Pres. Ronald, *49,* 87, 106
reconciliation. *See* Confession
religious discrimination
  by the Catholic Church, 36
  against Catholic politicians, 47,
      48, 85, 86
  against Catholics, 21, 22, 23,
      24–27, *26,* 42, 96
  watchdog against, 91
religious freedom, 20, 27, 50, 91
religious orders, 19, 54
Renwick, James, 42
resurrection of Jesus Christ, 8, 10
Ridge, Tom, 88
rituals. *See* practices; prayer
Roberts, Cokie, 37
Rockefeller Foundation, 103
Rodrique, William, 42
Roe v. Wade, 78, 79
Roman Catholic Church
  in America, 17, 117
  charities, 83
  creation, 15
Roman Empire, 7, 8, 11
Rome. *See* Pope; Vatican; Vatican II
Romero, 59
Roosevelt, Pres. Franklin D., 62, 88
Rosary and Altar Society, 25
rosary beads, 16–17, 28
Russert, Tim, 37
Russian Orthodox Church, 20, 25

sacraments
  and the Mass, 15–16
  the seven, 12
Saint Mary's City, 20
saints
  American, 101*t*
  role in Catholicism, 17
Santa Clara University, 56
Saul, 9
Scalia, Antonin, 70, 88, 103,
    106–107, *107*

Schuller, Robert, 62
seal of confession, 15
Second Vatican Council. *See* Vatican II
Selios, Father Francis X., 101*t*
Serbian Orthodox Church, 25
Serra, Father Junipero, 39, 40, 101*t*
Setaon, Saint Elizabeth, 101*t*
Seven Storey Mountain, The, 100
sex
  AIDS prevention, 77
  birth control, 76–77
  homosexuality, 69, 77–78
  pre-marital, 75
sexual offenses of priests, 113–114
Sheen, Fulton J. (bishop of Rochester), 62
Sheen, Martin, 37, 100, 105–106, *106*
Shrine of the Immaculate Conception, *33, 116*
Shriver, Maria, 103
sin, 8, 13, 15
Sisters of St. Joseph of Medaille, 104
Sisters of the Blessed Sacrament, 98
slavery, 21, 96
Smith, Al, 47, 85
soccer teams, 56
social activism, 91–93, 103–106
Social Development and World Peace, 89
social organizations, 25
Society of Jesus. *See* Jesuits
soup kitchens, *81–82,* 96, 99
Spain, 19, 39–40
sports teams, 56, 102
St. John's, 56
St. Mary's, 56
St. Patrick's Cathedral, *41,* 41–42
St. Patrick's Old Cathedral, 42, 97
statues, 28
stem cell research, 80

Stephanopoulos, George, 108
suicide, 80
"Survive," 105

Tagliabue, Paul, 103
Tekakwitha, Kateri, 101*t*
television, 62, 67, 91
Ten Commandments, The, 59
Teresa of Calcutta, Mother, 99
Texas, 28–29, 37*t,* 86
Thailand, 37
Thomas, Clarence, 88, 107
Toole, John Kennedy, 66
transubstantiation, 15, *16*
Trappists, 100
Twelve Apostles, 8, 11

UndUSA, 63
unions, 71, 88
United Nations General Assembly, 50
United States
  American saints, 101*t*
  colonial period, 19–21
  number of nuns and priests, 112, 112*f*
  percent of population Catholic, 37
  pre-colonial period, 19
  relationship of Catholics to Rome, 17
  top ten Catholic states, 37*t*
United States Catholic Miscellany, 60
United States Conference of Catholic Bishops (USCCB), 43, 89–90, 101
universal church, 17
University of Notre Dame, 56, 102–103
University of San Francisco, 56
U.S. Congress, 24, 43, 87, 106
U.S. Constitution, 27
U.S. Supreme Court, 88, 103, 106–107

Vatican
  ambassador to the, 87
  appointment of bishops, 21
  conflicts with the, 27–28
  Internet site, *64,* 64–65
  on the National Catholic War Council, 43
  on racial discrimination, 32–33
  relationship to American Catholics, 17, 24, 26, 117
  on slavery, 21
  on the use of the Internet, 65
  World Youth Day, 118
Vatican II, 30, 44–47, *45,* 111
victims' rights, 104–105
videos, 77
Vietnamese Catholics, 36–37, 117
Vietnam War, 36, 103
Vincent of Lerins, 117
Violent Bear it Away, The, 66

Walsh, William, 103
Wanderer, The, 60, 61
war
  praying for peace, 92–93, 104
  and weapons, 72, *73,* 92, 105, 106
Watson, Paul, 105
Weakland, Rembert (archbishop of Milwaukee), 71
Web. *See* Internet
Western division, 15
"What would Jesus do?", 67
Williams, Roger, 20
workers' rights, 71, 88, 89, 101–102
World Council of Churches, 25
World War I, 42–43
World War II, 44, 62–63
World Youth Day, 118

Xavier University, 98

Yardstick, The, 101